Polygons
Galore!

a mathematics unit for high-ability learners in grades 3–5

Polygons Galore!

Dana T. Johnson, Marguerite M. Mason, Ph.D., and Jill Adelson, Ph.D.

The College of William and Mary
School of Education
Center for Gifted Education
P.O. Box 8795
Williamsburg, VA 23187

Center for Gifted Education Staff:
Executive Director: Dr. Tracy L. Cross
Curriculum Director: Dr. Kimberley L. Chandler
Curriculum Writers: Dana T. Johnson,
Dr. Marguerite M. Mason, and Dr. Jill Adelson

Edited by Sean Redmond

Production design by Raquel Trevino

ISBN-13: 978-1-61821-021-0

Prufrock Press Inc.
P.O. Box 8813
Waco, TX 76714-8813
Phone: (800) 998-2208
Fax: (800) 240-0333
http://www.prufrock.com

Contents

Part I: Introduction

Introduction to the Unit 3

Assessment 4

Unit Glossary 5

Part II: Background for Teachers

The van Hiele Levels of Geometric Understanding 10

Part III: Lesson Plans

Preassessment 14

Lesson 1: Classifying Triangles.. 21

Lesson 2: Properties of Quadrilaterals 31

Lesson 3: Areas of Triangles 45

Lesson 4: Areas of Parallelograms and Kites............................... 57

Lesson 5: Areas of Trapezoids 70

Lesson 6: Perimeter vs. Area in Rectangles 77

Lesson 7: Polygon Patterns... 81

Lesson 8: The Particulars of Polyhedra 89

Lesson 9: Geometry Beyond the Textbook 96

Postassessment 102

References 109

About the Authors... 111

Part I: Introduction

Introduction to the Unit

Unit Description: *Polygons Galore!* investigates two-dimensional and three-dimensional components of geometry by exploring polygons and polyhedra and their properties.

Unit Rationale: Geometry is a fundamental and powerful strand of mathematics, and the foundation for spatial reasoning. Typical curriculum materials address geometry in a rote method that emphasizes recalling shapes and memorizing formulas. This unit goes beyond those methods by allowing students to:

- identify, compare, and analyze polygons by using properties of the polygons;
- construct meanings for geometric terms;
- develop strategies to find areas of specific polygons;
- identify and build regular and nonregular polyhedra;
- analyze the relationship of the numbers of vertices, faces, and edges in a polyhedron; and
- recognize geometric ideas and relationships as applied to other disciplines, such as art.

Differentiation for Gifted Learners: This unit gives students a much broader and deeper experience with geometry than do most curriculum materials. It is challenging in that it requires deep understanding of the mathematical strand of geometry rather than merely memorizing formulas and definitions or recognizing shapes. Reasons to use this unit with gifted learners include the following:

- The regular school curriculum at this level does not generally probe geometry beyond lines, area, and perimeter. This unit provides additional content experiences.
- Developing formulas for specific attributes of geometric shapes requires a much deeper understanding of the algorithms and serious thinking.
- Constructing meanings for mathematical terms mandates that the learner develop spatial thinking.
- Task demands are more strenuous than in typical curriculum materials. Students are frequently asked to complete tasks with less teacher support than would be given in a typical math class.
- Much of the work in this unit is inquiry-based. Although this approach may benefit all students, inquiry lessons are a good approach to unleash the thinking abilities of gifted students.
- The pace and density of material requires the ability to process concepts rapidly.

Links to Common Core State Standards and NCTM Standards: The Common Core State Standards for Mathematics (CCSSM) call for the study of geometry in grades K–12. As the CCSSM note: "Through building, drawing, and analyzing two- and three-dimensional shapes, students develop a foundation for understanding area, volume, congruence, similarity, and symmetry in later grades" (Common Core State Standards Initiative, 2010, p. 17). According to the CCSSM, by the fifth grade students understand that attributes belonging to a category of figures also belong to all subcategories of that category and can classify two-dimensional figures in a hierarchy based on properties. By sixth grade, students are finding the area of special quadrilaterals by composing into rectangles or decomposing into triangles and other polygons. This unit will provide the students with the means to investigate the geometric properties of figures and the relationships among various figures.

The National Council of Teachers of Mathematics' (NCTM, 2000) *Principals and Standards for School Mathematics* include the following for grades 3–5: "The reasoning skills that students develop in grades 3–5 allow them to investigate geometric problems of increasing complexity and to study geometric properties" (p. 165). This unit will not only allow students to study increasingly complex geometric shapes, but also afford them the opportunity to consider the various properties of those shapes and apply them to another discipline, specifically the visual arts.

Suggested Grade Level Range: 3–5, but the unit can be adapted to both older and younger students.

Prerequisite Knowledge:
- Familiarity with basic polygons such as triangles and quadrilaterals and their attributes.
- Proficiency with tasks involving sorting and classifying.
- Proficiency with rulers and protractors and/or angle rulers.

Length of Lessons: Some of the lessons can be done in 45 minutes whereas others may take two 45-minute sessions. These lessons can be customized by lengthening or omitting various activities.

Timing: This unit could be completed within 2 weeks, spread out throughout the semester, or done in a pull-out enrichment class. Not all lessons need to be included and the order of the later lessons may be determined by the teacher. It is recommended that Lessons 1, 2, 3, and 6 be included. The most serious and substantive treatment of the material will include all of the lessons and some of the extensions.

Extensions: Suggestions for extension activities are included within the lessons. Extensions can be done by groups or individually. You might also keep a piece of chart paper in your classroom and encourage students to generate questions for further study. Individuals or student groups can be assigned questions and report to the class on findings of additional extension activities. The extensions often require students to function somewhat independently. However, you may choose to assign an extension to less able students by writing a more scaffolded version of the task. The extensions will provide some opportunities to offer greater engagement to individuals who need extra challenges.

Assessment

Each lesson has suggested assessments, but teachers will find many more ways to determine student understanding.

Math Journals: If students maintain a math journal, they can be asked to solve a single problem in the journal and explain their reasoning. A good technique to give students an audience for their writing is to suggest that they are to write a postcard to a friend who has asked for help in solving the problem.

Preassessment: This is not a readiness test. You should administer it before you start the unit. It assumes that students know something about geometry. It is intended to give the teacher a baseline indicator of what students know before they begin work on the unit. Typically, they should not do well on the preassessment. (However, if they do know the material, be sure to assign appropriate extensions from the lessons.)

Postassessment: This is included at the end of the unit. You should administer it after you complete the unit. You are welcome to add any questions to both the pre- and postassessments.

Unit Glossary

Acute triangle: A triangle that has three acute angles (less than 90°).

Adjacent sides: Two sides that are side-by-side and share a common vertex.

Angle: The figure formed by two rays that share a common endpoint.

Archimedean solids: Solids made of two or more different regular polygons; semi-regular solids.

Area: The amount of surface of a region or shape (measured in square units).

Base of a triangle: Any one of the three sides of the triangle; usually the one drawn at the bottom, parallel to the floor.

Bisect: To cut into two equal parts.

Circle: A closed plane (two-dimensional) figure with all points of the figure equidistant (the same distance) from the center.

Congruent: Having the same size and shape.

Convex: Curving or bending outward (a convex polygon has no angles larger than 180 degrees).

Concave: Curving or bending inward (a concave polygon has at least one angle larger than 180 degrees).

Cube: A three-dimensional shape with six congruent square faces (it has 12 congruent edges and eight vertices or corners).

Cylinder: A three-dimensional shape with bases that are parallel, congruent circles.

Dart: A concave quadrilateral.

Decagon: A polygon with 10 sides.

Diagonal: A segment that joins two non consecutive vertices in a polygon or polyhedron.

Dodecagon: A polygon with 12 sides.

Dodecahedron: A polyhedron with 12 pentagonal faces.

Edge: A line segment where two faces of a three-dimensional figure meet.

Equilateral triangle: A triangle with three congruent sides and angles (each angle measures 60°); note that an equilateral triangle is a special case of an isosceles triangle.

Face: A flat side of a three-dimensional figure (a face will be a polygon).

Geometry: The branch of mathematics that deals with position, size, and shape of figures.

Height of a triangle: The perpendicular distance of the vertex (that is opposite to the base side) from the line containing the base.

Heptagon: A polygon with seven sides.

Hexagon: A polygon with six sides.

Hexahedron: A polyhedron with six faces (if the faces are squares, it is a cube).

Icosahedron: A polyhedron with 20 triangular faces.

Isosceles triangle: A triangle with at least two equal sides and angles (note that an equilateral triangle is a special case of an isosceles triangle).

Kite: A convex quadrilateral with two pairs of congruent adjacent sides but all four sides are not congruent.

Net: A two-dimensional pattern that forms a polyhedron when folded into a three-dimensional shape.

Nonagon: A polygon with nine sides.

Obtuse triangle: A triangle with one obtuse angle (greater than 90° and less than 180°).

Octagon: A polygon with eight sides.

Octahedron: A polyhedron with eight faces.

Opposite angles: In a quadrilateral, angles that do not have a common line segment.

Parallel lines: Two or more lines in a plane that are always the same distance apart and never intersect.

Parallelogram: A quadrilateral with opposite sides parallel and congruent (opposite angles are congruent).

Pentagon: A polygon with five sides.

Perimeter: The distance around the outside of a two-dimensional shape.

Perpendicular lines: Lines that meet at right angles.

Platonic solids: The five regular polyhedra.

Polygon: Two-dimensional, closed figure made up of three or more line segments that do not intersect except at endpoints of the segments.

Polyhedron: A solid made of polygonal faces.

Prism: A three-dimensional figure with bases that are parallel and congruent; these bases are joined by parallelograms.

Quadrilateral: A polygon with four sides.

Rectangle: A parallelogram with four right angles.

Regular polygon: A polygon that has all congruent sides and congruent angles.

Regular polyhedron: A polyhedron that has faces that are congruent polygons; also called Platonic solids.

Rhombus: A parallelogram with four congruent sides (plural: rhombuses or rhombi).

Right angle: An angle that measures 90°.

Right triangle: A triangle that has one right angle (90°).

Scalene triangle: A triangle that has no congruent sides.

Square: A rectangle with equal sides.

Square unit: A unit that has equal length and width, used to measure area.

Tetrahedron: A polyhedron with four triangular faces.

Three-dimensional: Having three dimensions: length, width, and depth (or breadth).

Trapezoid: A quadrilateral with exactly one pair of parallel sides.

Triangle: A polygon with three sides.

Vertex: A point where sides of a shape, rays of an angle, or edges of a solid meet; also called a corner in some textbooks (plural: vertices).

Part II: Background for Teachers

The van Hiele Levels of Geometric Understanding

Pierre van Hiele and Dina van Hiele-Geldof conceptualized developmental spatial reasoning along a sequential continuum. The levels, although sequential in nature, are not age specific; rather, they are based on relevant geometric experiences. They represent the stage of understanding that a student has attained. There are six levels, numbered 0–5. Table 1 explains the levels and the abilities associated with each.

Some of the activities in this unit require students to function at the Analysis (Level 2) and Abstraction (Level 3) levels. The early activities will help ensure that students advance to Level 3, but if you notice students who are still working from pictures in their heads rather than properties, you will need to pay careful attention to them, as they are still thinking at Level 1. They will require more activities and questioning from you to move forward.

According to the van Hiele theory, students cannot think at a higher level without mastering all of the previous levels. However, some gifted students will be able to understand and make logical implications based on incorrect definitions. This reasoning ability has been acquired in areas other than geometry and they are applying it to geometry. They will appear to skip levels and are the only population to do so. The students will be applying correct reasoning to faulty concepts. This is one reason why it is so important to be sure that the students have a rich understanding of the definitions and attributes of figures to provide the foundation for their advanced levels of thinking.

Typically, the process used to help students move upward in their developmental levels occurs in phases such as these:

1. **Inquiry:** This is exemplified in the triangle sorting task in Lesson 1. Hands-on activities are important in this process, rather than just teacher demonstration or presentation of definitions.
2. **Guided orientation:** The teacher provides experiences that involve looking for the desired relationships.
3. **Explanation:** Students use words to describe the ideas they have been experiencing. This is why discussion is important after students complete hands-on activities.
4. **Free orientation:** Students apply their understanding of concepts to more complex tasks.
5. **Integration:** Students summarize what they have learned about a concept.

For more information on the van Hiele levels of geometric understanding, see:

Crowley, M. L. (1987). The van Hiele model of the development of geometric thought. In M. M. Lindquist (Ed.), *Learning and teaching geometry, K–12* (pp. 1–16). Reston, VA: National Council of Teachers of Mathematics.

Mason, M. (1997). The van Hiele model of geometric understanding and mathematically talented students. *Journal for the Education of the Gifted, 21*, 38–53.

Van Hiele, P. M. (1999). Developing geometric thinking through activities that begin with play. *Teaching Children Mathematics, 5*, 310–316.

Table 1

The van Hiele Levels of Geometric Understanding

Level Number	Name	Description
0	Pre-recognition	Geometric figures are not recognized. For example, students cannot differentiate between three-sided and four-sided polygons.
1	Visualization	Students functioning at this level can recognize and name a shape such as a triangle based upon their knowledge of a triangle image. However, if the picture of a triangle is flipped so the base is at the top and the vertex is pointed downward, this student may not call it a triangle, because it does not exactly match the picture the student has in his or her head. The student is working from mental images, not definitions or properties of the shape.
2	Analysis	This level is characterized by student ability to identify characteristics of shapes and correctly use vocabulary related to the characteristics. For example, a student at Level 2 may correctly identify a triangle because it has three sides and three angles. However, the student might not be able to perceive that a figure having three angles is sufficient to make the figure a triangle.
3	Abstraction (or Informal Deduction)	Students at this level can recognize relationships between and among properties of shapes and are able to articulate reasons for classifying in certain ways. For example, a student may be able to compare the right angle of a triangle with the right angles of a rectangle. Logical implications (e.g., "if a quadrilateral is a square, then it is a rectangle") and class inclusions (e.g., "every rectangle is a parallelogram because it is just a special parallelogram with right angles") can be understood.
4	Deduction	Students at this level can construct proofs and understand the role of axioms and definitions. In order to be successful in high school geometry, students need to be functioning at this level.
5	Rigor	This level involves students working in non-Euclidean geometric systems. A student should understand the role and necessity of indirect proof and proof by contrapositive.

Part III: Lesson Plans

Preassessment
Lesson 1: Classifying Triangles
Lesson 2: Properties of Quadrilaterals
Lesson 3: Areas of Triangles
Lesson 4: Areas of Parallelograms and Kites
Lesson 5: Areas of Trapezoids
Lesson 6: Perimeter vs. Area in Rectangles
Lesson 7: Polygon Patterns
Lesson 8: The Particulars of Polyhedra
Lesson 9: Geometry Beyond the Textbook
Postassessment

Preassessment

Instructional Purpose

- To assess student knowledge and understanding of unit topics.

Materials and Handouts

- Preassessment
- Preassessment Answer Key

Activities

1. Before starting the unit, administer the preassessment to determine the extent of student understanding of the concepts that are addressed in this unit. Distribute the **Preassessment** and have students complete it individually.

2. Collect and score the preassessment using the **Preassessment Answer Key.**

Notes to Teacher

- You may want to reassure your students that they are not expected to know the answers to these items before they complete the unit. At the end of the unit they will take a parallel form of the test as a postassessment. By comparing the scores, you will be able to see where students have gained in their knowledge of geometric concepts.
- This is not a timed test. You may allow whatever time is needed by your students to provide a response to every item.
- The preassessment is not passed back to students upon completion.

Preassessment

Directions: Do your best to answer the following questions.

1. Describe as many of each triangle's properties as you can.

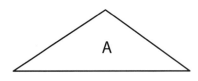

2. Group these triangles in any way you choose. Write the letters of the triangles in each group. Explain why you grouped them the way you did.

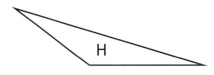

3. Mario uses three sticks to make a triangle. One stick is 11 inches long. Another is 8 inches long. What is true about the length of the third stick?

4. Given the figures at right, write the letter of each that is a:

    a. quadrilateral _____

    b. rectangle _____

    c. parallelogram _____

    d. rhombus _____

    e. trapezoid _____

    f. kite _____

    g. square _____

    h. dart _____

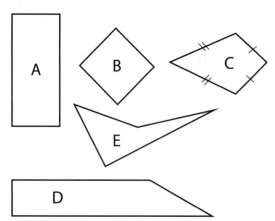

5. Without using a formula, find the area of this parallelogram. Explain your thinking.

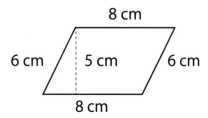

6. Look at this geometric figure.

    a. Is this figure a polygon? Explain why or why not.

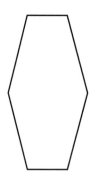

    b. Is it regular? Explain why or why not.

    c. What special name does this shape have?

7. A picture of a polyhedron is shown.

   a. How many faces does it have? _____

   b. How many vertices does it have? _____

   c. How many edges does it have? _____

8. Which of the items listed below is a polygon? _____

   Which is a polyhedron? _____

   a. A can of soup
   b. The label from a can of soup
   c. A cereal box
   d. The front of a cereal box

Preassessment Answer Key

Maximum possible points: 28

1. **(4 points)** Describe as many of the triangle's properties as you can.

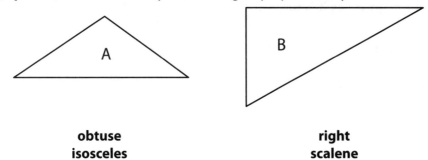

obtuse	**right**
isosceles	**scalene**

Give one point for each correct response.

2. **(4 points)** Group these triangles in any way you choose. Write the letters of the triangles in each group. Explain why you grouped them the way you did.

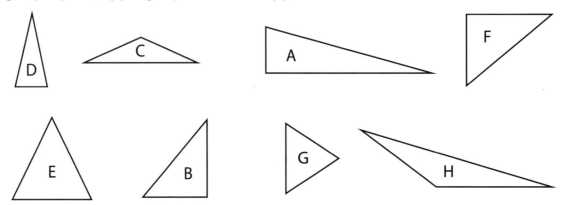

Many different groupings are possible. Each of the eight letters should be included in a group. The groups need not be labeled with technical terms but should have some description of what they have in common. Some examples of groupings are listed below.

Grouped by angles:	**Grouped by whether it has a right angle or not:**	**Grouped by sides:**
A, B, F (right triangles) D, E, G (acute triangles) C, H (obtuse triangles)	A, B, F (has a right angle) C, D, E, G, H (has no right angle)	E, G (three congruent sides) B, C, D, F, H (two congruent sides) A (no congruent sides)

- **Give 4 points** if reasonable grouping is used, explanation of groups is given, terminology is correct, and all eight triangles are included in one group each.
- **Give 3 points** if groupings seem to be made based on characteristics of the triangles such as sides or angles but one of these is a problem:
  - one or more triangles are left out,
  - there is no adequate labeling of groups or explanation,
  - terminology is primitive or incorrect (e.g., "square corners" instead of "right angles"), or
  - the same triangle is included in more than one category.

- **Give 2 points** if the groupings are made based on visual characteristics such as "large and small" or "pointing right and pointing left" rather than using geometric terms as sorting categories.
- **Give 1 point** if there is minimal evidence of a sorting rule used but it is not totally correct or complete.
- **Give 0 points** if there is no response or if the student seems confused. Give 0 points if the sort is done by letters such as the vowels and consonants that are used to label them.

3. **(3 points)** Mario uses three sticks to make a triangle. One stick is 11 inches long. Another is 8 inches long. What can you say about the length of the third stick?
It must be more than 3 inches and less than 19 inches.

4. **(4 points)** Given the figures at right, write the letter of each that is a:
   a. quadrilateral **A, B, C, D, E**
   b. rectangle **A, B**
   c. parallelogram **A, B**
   d. rhombus **B**
   e. trapezoid **D**
   f. kite **C**
   g. square **B**
   h. dart **E**

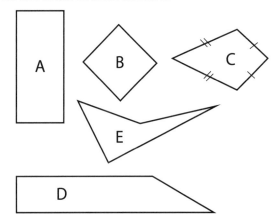

Note: Please see the glossary for definitions of these quadrilaterals if you need them.

5. **(3 points)** Without using a formula, find the area of this parallelogram. Explain your thinking.

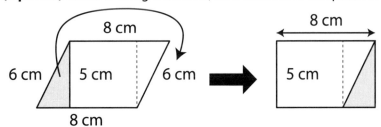

The area is 40 square cm. Move the triangle on the left to the right as shown and find the area of the rectangle or add the area of the two triangles to the area of the smaller rectangle.

6. **(3 points)** Look at this geometric figure.
    a. Is this figure a polygon? Explain why or why not.
        Yes, it satisfies the definition of a polygon because it is made of more than two line segments that do not intersect (except at endpoints), it lies in a plane, and it is closed.
    b. Is it regular? Explain why or why not.
        No. Not all of the sides and angles have the same measure.
    c. What special name does this shape have?
        Hexagon

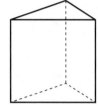

7. **(3 points)** A picture of a polyhedron is shown.
    a. How many faces does it have?
        5 faces
    b. How many vertices does it have?
        6 vertices
    c. How many edges does it have?
        9 edges

8. **(4 points)** Which of the items listed below is a polygon? **b, d**
    Which is a polyhedron? **c**
    a. A can of soup
    b. The label from a can of soup
    c. A cereal box
    d. The front of a cereal box

Lesson 1: Classifying Triangles

Instructional Purpose

- To sort and classify different types of triangles using one or more properties.
- To correctly name a triangle using one or more of its properties.
- To determine that the sum of any two sides of a triangle must be greater than the length of the third side.

Materials and Handouts

- Rulers
- A 3" x 5" card for each student
- Straws or pieces of spaghetti cut to the following lengths: 3", 4", 5", 6" (for teacher use)
- Packets of uncut straws or spaghetti for pairs of students
- Scissors
- Clear tape
- Dictionaries
- Vocabulary Word Study (Handout 1A)
- Triangles (Handout 1B)
- Triangle Record Keeping (Handout 1C)
- Lesson 1 Summary (Handout 1D)

Activities

1. Introduce the unit and the lesson. This unit will study polygons and their relatives, polyhedrons. We will study the idea of polygons in more depth in a later lesson, but for now we will work from the idea that a polygon is a closed figure that can be drawn on a page with line segments.

   Ask students what the minimum number of sides must be to create a polygon. Use the answer "three" as a springboard to this lesson, with the study of the simplest polygon: the triangle.

2. Distribute dictionaries and the **Vocabulary Word Study (Handout 1A)**. Have students complete the worksheet for the word *triangle*.

3. Discuss students' Vocabulary Word Study pages and allow the students to add to them as needed. Ask students what parts of triangles mathematicians might use to describe different kinds of triangles (angles and sides). That is what we are going to do in this lesson—use different sides and angles to classify triangles.

4. Give students **Triangles (Handout 1B)**. Have them cut out the triangles. Ask them to sort the triangles into two or more groups and to write the letters of each group on a piece of paper or in their math journals. Ask students to mix the triangles, re-sort them in another way, and record the letters of the new groups. Have students share their sorts and explain their reasoning. As students tell about the characteristics of their groupings, review the names of the following properties: *acute, right, obtuse, scalene, isosceles, equilateral*. (These words may be found in the glossary at the end of Part I.) The terms may be new to some

students, so make sure to spend some time reinforcing them. Tell students that you will be using these terms to describe triangles in future activities. If students do not know these terms, introduce them and emphasize the use of accurate mathematical terms. For example, students might say that certain triangles have a square corner. Ask them to use the term *right triangle* instead.

5. Share results.

6. Distribute **Triangle Record Keeping (Handout 1C)** to students.

7. Give students rulers and pieces of uncut spaghetti or straws, 3" x 5" cards, and scissors. Have them snap the spaghetti or cut the straws into lengths of the following measurements: 3", 4", 5", and 6". Each student should make three of each length. (Note: The lengths may be color-coded using a marker for easy recognition later.)

8. Make a triangle on the overhead projector using pieces of lengths 3", 3", and 5". Ask students which terms can be used to describe the triangle. (Obtuse and isosceles; you may use the corner of a 3" x 5" card to check for the size of angles relative to a right angle.) Have students draw this example on Handout 1C in the appropriate place (middle cell of the fourth row) and label the side lengths.

9. Ask students to use their straws or spaghetti pieces and the 3" x 5" card to see if they can find an example of a triangle to put in the last box on the page—right and equilateral. It is impossible! So they should write "not possible" in that box. (Again, use the 3" x 5" card as an aid to check for a right angle.)

10. Ask students to make different triangles using exactly three spaghetti pieces as sides to match the required characteristics of the boxes in the handout. Have students draw and label side lengths of their triangles in the appropriate boxes of the handout. (Answers will vary, but note that certain triangles are not possible; see answer key.) Have students share their answers.

11. Ask: *How many different triangles can be made using only the length of sides we have here (3, 4, 5, and 6 inches)?* Debrief answers. (The following 19 different triangles are possible. Note that 3-3-6 is not possible; encourage students to try it and they should see the reason why those lengths do not work.)

3-3-3	4-4-3	5-5-3	6-6-3
3-3-4	4-4-4	5-5-4	6-6-4
3-3-5	4-4-5	5-5-5	6-6-5
3-4-5	4-4-6	5-5-6	6-6-6
3-4-6	4-5-6		
3-5-6			

12. Ask students if it is possible to make a triangle using more than three pieces. (It is, such as by taking 3", 4", 5", and 6" pieces, joining the 3" and 4" pieces to make a 7" piece, and then making a 5-6-7 triangle.) Ask students to make and record all of the triangles they can with four pieces of spaghetti. Emphasize to students

that, even though they may be using four pieces of spaghetti, they are only making three sides.

13. Ask students if there were any combinations they tried that did not form triangles. (3-3-6 is one example from Step 11; another example is 4-4-9 where the 9" piece is made from 3" and 6" pieces). Ask: *What makes these triangles impossible?* Nudge students toward a generalization that the sum of any two side-lengths of a triangle must be greater than the length of the third side of the triangle. (When they get to high school, the geometry textbook will call this *The Triangle Inequality*.)

14. If students are able, use some higher order questions such as these to probe relationships within triangles.
    - Given the following triangle, what can you say about the length of side *x*? (It must be more than 4 cm and less than 8 cm.) Students can experiment with spaghetti sticks.

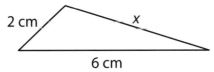

    - If the three sides of the triangle are different lengths (scalene triangle), where would you expect to find the largest angle? (Opposite the longest side) Where would you expect to find the smallest angle? (Opposite the shortest side)
    - True or false? If you make a right triangle, the longest side of the triangle is opposite the right angle. (True; in middle school and high school, this will be given the name *hypotenuse*.)

15. Have students complete the **Lesson 1 Summary (Handout 1D)**. Collect the papers and review student understanding.

Assessment
- Observations (class discussions)
- Triangle Record Keeping (Handout 1C)
- Lesson 1 Summary (Handout 1D)

Notes to Teacher
- Students will sort the triangles in different ways in Step 4. There is no correct way for the sorting to occur. The idea is for students to notice properties of triangles that are the same or different. In order to do this, they must be functioning at a van Hiele Level 2 or higher. If students sort the triangles by categories such as "big triangles" and "little triangles," it means that they are not yet seeing properties of triangles.
- Having students sort the triangles in more than one way pushes them to the limits of their thinking. Often they will do a first sort at a lower van Hiele level than the second sort. Students who can only do one sort are often functioning at a lower van Hiele level.
- Step 11, where students look for all of the possible triangles that can be made with the given side lengths, is a "fluency" activity. It is exploratory and some-

what open-ended as students do not know how many triangles there are and must develop strategies for testing all possibilities.

- You might want to show students the markings that are used in geometric figures to show which sides are the same length, as demonstrated in Figure 1.1.

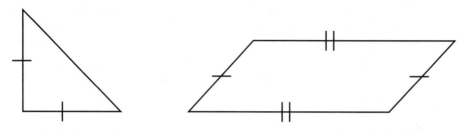

Figure 1.1. Markings indicating equal length.

- Watch for a misconception about right triangles in which students think right triangles are "pointing to the right" as in the triangle in Figure 1.1. Make sure you emphasize other orientations.
- Note that the definition of *isosceles triangle* is "a triangle with at least two congruent sides and angles." This means that an equilateral triangle is a special case of an isosceles triangle.

Extensions

- Ask students to use six straws or pieces of spaghetti and clear tape to create a three-dimensional structure. Have students use mathematical terms to identify any triangles that are seen on the faces (surfaces) of the structure.
- Triangular patterns can occur without using line segments. Consider the triangle of numbers shown in Figure 1.2. It is called Pascal's triangle (named for the French mathematician Blaise Pascal). Share this with your students and have them complete the following exercises:
  a. Write the next row of numbers in the triangle.
  b. What patterns do you see in Pascal's triangle?
  c. Circle the numbers that are divisible by 3. What pattern appears now?

Figure 1.2. Pascal's triangle.

Name: _____ Date: _____

Vocabulary Word Study (Handout 1A)

Term

Definition	Draw a Picture or Diagram

Real-World Example	Analyze the Word
	Language of origin: **Stems (parts of the word) and what they mean:** **Word families (other words with the same stem[s]):**

Name: _____   Date: _____

Triangles (Handout 1B)

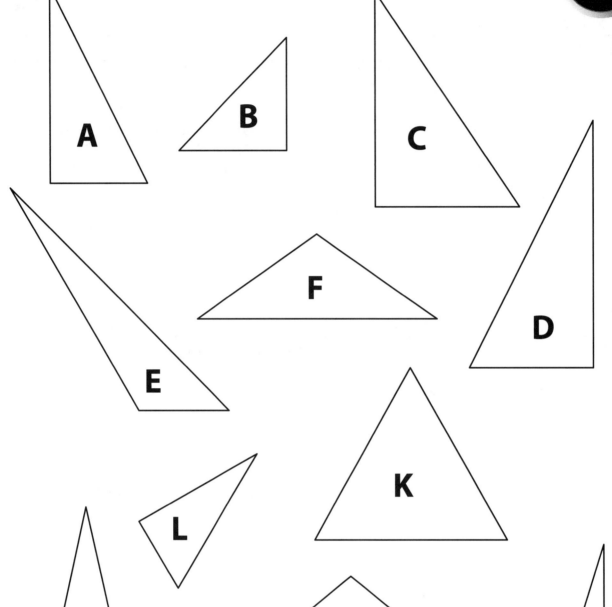

A   B   C

F   D

E

K

L

J   H

G   I

Triangle Record Keeping (Handout 1C)

Directions: Make an example of each type of triangle with your straw or spaghetti segments. Draw the results and label the lengths of the sides. If it is impossible to make, write "not possible."

Acute	Obtuse	Right
Scalene	**Isosceles**	**Equilateral**
Acute and Scalene	**Acute and Isosceles**	**Acute and Equilateral**
Obtuse and Scalene	**Obtuse and Isosceles**	**Obtuse and Equilateral**
Right and Scalene	**Right and Isosceles**	**Right and Equilateral**

Triangle Record Keeping
Answer Key (Teacher Resource 1)

Directions: Make an example of each type of triangle with your straw or spaghetti segments. Draw the results and label the lengths of the sides. If it is impossible to make, write "not possible."

Acute	Obtuse	Right
Examples: 4-5-6 3-5-5 All angles must be less than 90° (acute).	**Example:** 3-3-5 One angle must be greater than 90° (obtuse).	3-4-5 This is the only right triangle that can be made with the given lengths.
Scalene	**Isosceles**	**Equilateral**
Examples: 3-4-5 3-5-6 All sides have different measures.	**Example:** 4-6-6 At least two sides have the same measure.	**Example:** 4-4-4 All sides and angles have the same measures.
Acute and Scalene	**Acute and Isosceles**	**Acute and Equilateral**
Example: 4-5-6	**Example:** 3-5-5	**Example:** 3-3-3 Note: All equilateral triangles are acute, but not all acute triangles are equilateral.
Obtuse and Scalene	**Obtuse and Isosceles**	**Obtuse and Equilateral**
Example: 3-5-6	**Example:** 3-3-5	Not possible with the given lengths (or any lengths).
Right and Scalene	**Right and Isosceles**	**Right and Equilateral**
Example: 3-4-5	Not possible with the given lengths.	Not possible with the given lengths (or any lengths).

Name: _____ Date: _____

1. Describe each triangle by as many of its properties as you can. You may use terms from this list: *acute*, *right*, *obtuse*, *scalene*, *isosceles*, and *equilateral*.

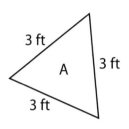

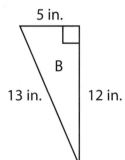

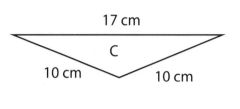

2. Mrs. Johnson made a drawing for a worksheet about triangles for her students. Then she noticed an error.
   a. What is the error?

   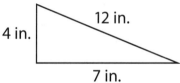

   b. Explain why this is a problem.

3. These triangle groupings were made by some properties of the triangles. What properties were used to sort the triangles into these groups?

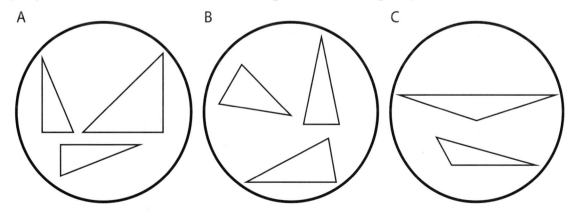

_____ _____ _____

Lesson 1 Summary Answer Key (Teacher Resource 2)

1. Describe each triangle by as many of its properties as you can. You may use terms from this list: *acute, right, obtuse, scalene, isosceles,* and *equilateral.*

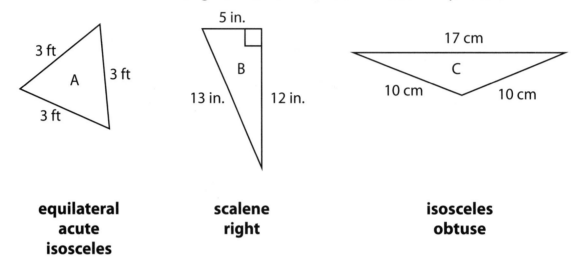

equilateral
acute
isosceles

scalene
right

isosceles
obtuse

2. Mrs. Johnson made a drawing for a worksheet about triangles for her students. Then she noticed an error.
   a. What is the error?
      The error is that 12 inches is too long for the longest side (or one of the other sides is too short).

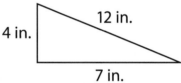

   b. Explain why this is a problem.
      No one side can be longer than the sum of the other two sides.

3. These triangle groupings were made by some properties of the triangles. What properties were used to sort the triangles into these groups?

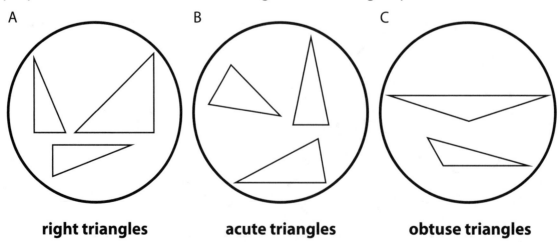

right triangles

acute triangles

obtuse triangles

Lesson 2: Properties of Quadrilaterals

Instructional Purpose

- To classify and describe quadrilaterals according to their properties.
- To identify, compare, and analyze attributes of quadrilaterals.

Materials and Handouts

- Sandwich bags for storage of cut pieces (one per student)
- Protractors and/or angle rulers
- Scissors
- Dictionaries
- A 3" x 5" card for each student
- Vocabulary Word Study (Handout 2A)
- Quadrilateral Sorting Pieces (Handout 2B) (2 sheets)
- Multiple Quadrilateral Sort (Handout 2C)
- Quadrilateral Sorting Table (Handout 2D)
- Types of Quadrilaterals (Handout 2E)
- Lesson 2 Summary (Handout 2F)

Activities

1. Distribute dictionaries and give each student two copies of the **Vocabulary Word Study (Handout 2A)**. On the first sheet, have students complete the activity for the word *quadrilateral*.

2. Review the following vocabulary for this lesson. Assign these terms to student pairs (one each) and have them complete a Vocabulary Word Study. Each pair should teach their word definition to the class. You may want to post the words on the class bulletin board for the remainder of the unit study.
   - right angle
   - parallel lines
   - perpendicular lines
   - adjacent sides
   - congruent sides
   - diagonal of a quadrilateral
   - concave
   - convex
   - bisect
   - congruent angles

3. Ask students to carefully cut out the pieces from **Quadrilateral Sorting Pieces (Handout 2B).** Although students will be working in pairs, each student should have his or her own set of pieces.

4. Distribute the **Multiple Quadrilateral Sort (Handout 2C)**. Have students sort the quadrilaterals in any way they wish and complete the worksheet. Debrief, having students share their multiple sorts.

5. Working in pairs, have students spread out their quadrilateral sets with the letters facing up so that they can easily be seen. Distribute the **Quadrilateral Sorting Table (Handout 2D)**. Ask student pairs to find all of the quadrilaterals in the set that have four *right angles*. Pairs need to agree on their selections and be able to justify them to each other. Students should measure the angles of the quadrilaterals with a protractor or angle ruler, but may use a 3" x 5" card as a guide to verify right angles. Pairs should write the letters of all of the quadrilaterals that have four right angles on the first line of the Quadrilateral Sorting Table (Handout 2D).

6. Have students consider the quadrilaterals again. Ask them to find all of the quadrilaterals that have exactly one pair of parallel sides. Pairs should agree on their selections and be able to justify their choices to each other. They should enter their answers on Line 2 of the Quadrilateral Sorting Table (Handout 2D).

7. Ask students to continue sorting and classifying quadrilaterals in this manner until the second column of the table is complete. When students are finished, have them come together for a whole-class discussion and check of their results.

8. Write the terms *quadrilateral, parallelogram, rectangle, rhombus, square, dart,* and *trapezoid* on the board, overhead projector, or document camera. Distribute copies of **Types of Quadrilaterals (Handout 2E)** as a resource. Explain that these are the terms that are used to label quadrilaterals by their properties. Discuss each term and ask students to find examples from their sorting pieces. Then have groups work on the third column of the Quadrilateral Sorting Table (Handout 2D) with the most specific proper term that describes the identified group. When they are finished, ask them to compare their answers with a partner. Discuss as a whole class.

9. Have a class discussion using the following questions:
   - Is every rectangle a parallelogram? (Yes) Is every parallelogram a rectangle? (No)
   - Is every square a rhombus? (Yes) Is every rhombus a square? (No)
   - Is every square a rectangle? (Yes) Is every rectangle a square? (No)
   - Can a dart have a right angle? (Yes, but only one)
   - I am thinking of a quadrilateral that has two right angles. What could it be? (Square, rectangle, or trapezoid)
   - I am thinking of a closed shape with four sides where no two of the sides are the same length. What could the shape be? (Trapezoid or dart)

10. Ask students to create a graphic organizer showing the relationships of the various types of quadrilaterals. You may suggest a Venn diagram or tree diagram format. This can be done as a whole-class discussion or done independently by groups. Two examples are included: **Venn Diagram of Quadrilateral Relationships (Teacher Resource 2)** and **Flow Diagram of Quadrilateral Relationships (Teacher Resource 3).**

11. Have students store their pieces in their sandwich bags, then complete **Lesson 2 Summary (Handout 2F)** and discuss.

Assessment

- Observations (class discussions, partner work); probe for understanding of properties of quadrilaterals

- Quadrilateral Sorting Table (Handout 2D)
- Lesson 2 Summary (Handout 2F)

Notes to Teacher

- The plural of rhombus is either rhombuses or rhombi.
- Some geometric terms such as trapezoid and kite have slightly different definitions in different parts of the world. The definitions given in Handout 2E are the traditional definitions used in textbooks in the United States.
- Sometimes students think that a diagonal can only be inside of a polygon. However, in a concave polygon such as a dart, it may fall outside the quadrilateral as shown in Figure 2.1.

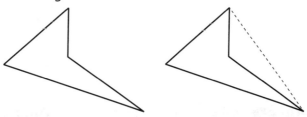

Figure 2.1. External diagonal of a concave polygon.

- Many students have only seen Venn diagrams as two overlapping circles that are used in a "compare and contrast" activity. The use of Venn diagrams in this lesson where some sets of shapes are entirely contained within another set might be a new idea for students.
- If you choose to use the Flow Diagram of Quadrilateral Relationships (Teacher Resource 3), you may use a phrase to indicate that each arrow means "is a subset of," "belongs to," or "is part of" the category above it.
- Students must be functioning at van Hiele Level 3 (Abstraction) to be able to understand that some quadrilateral groups satisfy the properties for other quadrilateral groups (e.g., every square is a rectangle). If you notice that a student does not recognize Quadrilateral E in Quadrilateral Sorting Pieces (Handout 2B) as a square because it is oriented in a way that does not look like the picture of a square that is usually presented in textbooks (sitting on an edge), that student is functioning at van Hiele Level 1.
- The purpose of multiple sortings of the quadrilaterals is to force students to look at properties beyond their initial impression. If students can only sort in one way, they are functioning at a lower van Hiele level than students who can sort in more than one way.
- An angle ruler is a tool for measuring angles. It is an easier tool for students to use than a protractor. If students have not used one before, you may have to allow time for them to try it.

Name: _____ Date: _____

Vocabulary Word Study (Handout 2A)

Term

Definition	Draw a Picture or Diagram

Real-World Example	Analyze the Word
	Language of origin: **Stems (parts of the word) and what they mean:** **Word families (other words with the same stem[s]):**

Quadrilateral Sorting Pieces (Handout 2B)

A

B

C

D

E

F

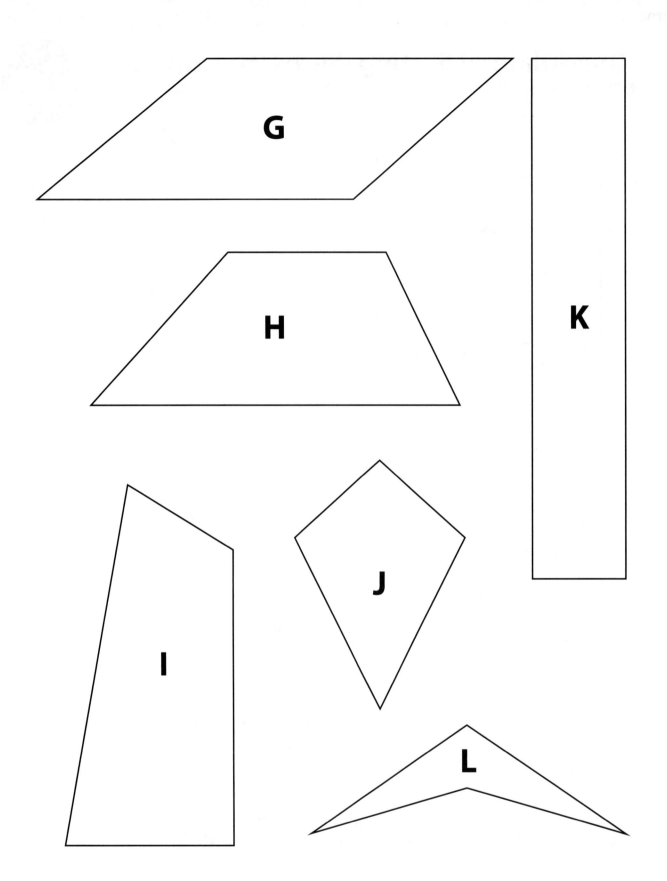

Multiple Quadrilateral Sort (Handout 2C)

The quadrilaterals that you cut out may be grouped together in many different ways.

1. Sort them into groups that belong together. Record the letters of the pieces you put together and write the reason that you think they belong together.

2. Mix the pieces and sort them again in a different way. Record the letters of the pieces you put together and write the reason that you think they belong together.

3. Can you think of a third way to sort the pieces? If so, sort them again and record the letters of the pieces you put together and write the reason that you think they belong together.

Name: _____ Date: _____

Quadrilateral Sorting Table (Handout 2D)

Directions: Use the quadrilaterals you cut out from Handout 2B to complete this table.

Sort All Pieces . . .	List the Pieces by Letter	Most Specific Label for This/These Figure(s)
1. that have four right angles.		
2. that have exactly one pair of parallel sides.		
3. that have two pairs of opposite sides congruent.		
4. that have four congruent sides.		
5. that have two pairs of opposite sides parallel.		
6. that have no congruent sides.		
7. that have two pairs of adjacent sides congruent, but not all sides congruent.		
8. that have perpendicular diagonals.		
9. that have opposite angles congruent.		
10. that are concave.		
11. that are convex.		
12. whose diagonals bisect one another.		
13. that have four sides.		
14. that have four congruent angles.		
15. that have four congruent sides and four congruent angles.		

Quadrilateral Sorting Table Answer Key (Teacher Resource 1)

Directions: Use the quadrilaterals you cut out from Handout 2B to complete this table.

Sort All Pieces . . .	List the Pieces by Letter	Most Specific Label for This/These Figure(s)
1. that have four right angles.	A, D, E, K	rectangle
2. that have exactly one pair of parallel sides.	F, H	trapezoid
3. that have two pairs of opposite sides congruent.	A, B, D, E, G, K	parallelogram
4. that have four congruent sides.	A, B, E	rhombus
5. that have two pairs of opposite sides parallel.	A, B, D ,E ,G, K	parallelogram
6. that have no congruent sides.	C, F, H, I	quadrilateral
7. that have two pairs of adjacent sides congruent, but not all sides congruent.	J, L	kite or dart
8. that have perpendicular diagonals.	A, B, E, J (and L if you draw the exterior diagonal and the short one appears perpendicular to it)	kite or rhombus (L is a dart)
9. that have opposite angles congruent.	A, B, D, E, G, K	parallelogram
10. that are concave.	C, L	dart
11. that are convex.	A, B, D, E, F, G, H, I, J, K	quadrilateral or convex quadrilateral
12. whose diagonals bisect one another.	A, B, D, E, G, J, K	parallelogram or kite
13. that have four sides.	A, B, C, D, E, F, G, H, I, J, K, L (all)	quadrilateral
14. that have four congruent angles.	A, D, E, K	rectangle
15. that have four congruent sides and four congruent angles.	A, E	square

Name: _____ Date: _____

Types of Quadrilaterals (Handout 2E)

A **quadrilateral** is a **four**-sided polygon.

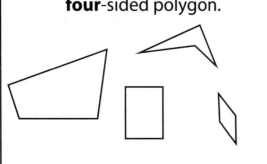

A **parallelogram** is a quadrilateral with both pairs of **opposite** sides **parallel**.

These sides are parallel

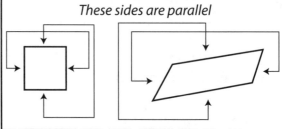

A **rectangle** is a quadrilateral with **four right angles**.

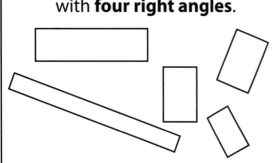

A **rhombus** is a quadrilateral with **four sides congruent**.

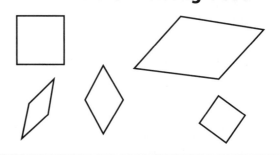

A **square** is a quadrilateral with **four right angles** and **four congruent sides**.

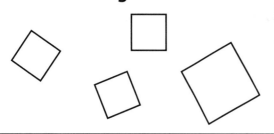

A **trapezoid** is a quadrilateral with **exactly one** pair of parallel sides.

These sides are parallel

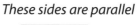
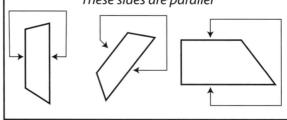

A **kite** is a convex quadrilateral with two distinct pairs of **adjacent congruent sides**.

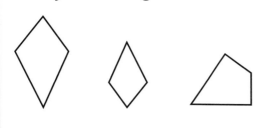

A **dart** is a **concave** quadrilateral.

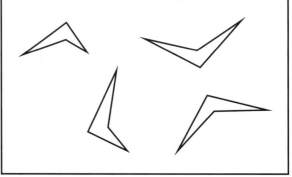

Venn Diagram of Quadrilateral Relationships (Teacher Resource 2)

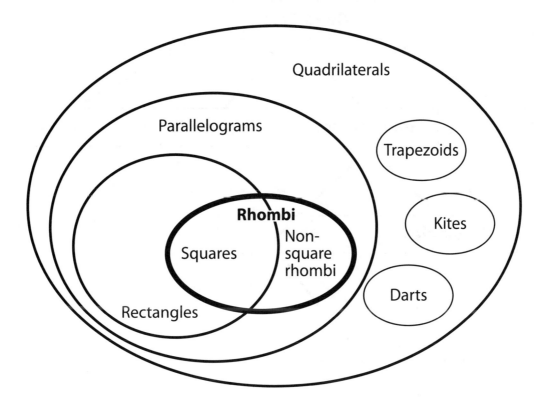

Flow Diagram of Quadrilateral Relationships (Teacher Resource 3)

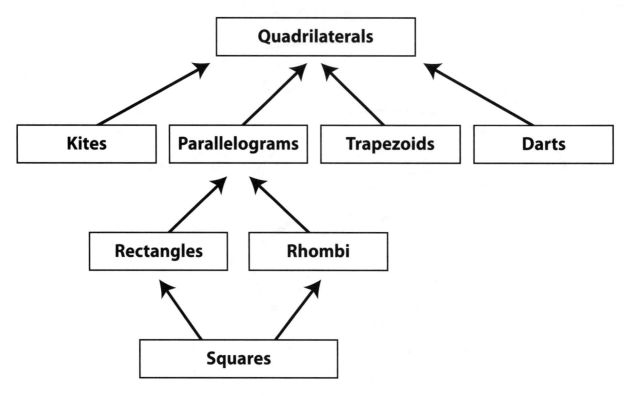

Name: _____ Date: _____

Lesson 2 Summary (Handout 2F)

1. Check all properties that always apply to each shape.

	Opposite Sides Parallel	Four Congruent Sides	Opposite Sides Congruent	Opposite Angles Congruent	Four Congruent Angles	Four Right Angles
Quadrilateral						
Rectangle						
Parallelogram						
Square						
Rhombus						
Trapezoid						
Kite						
Dart						

2. True or false? If the answer is false, show a counterexample.

   a. If a parallelogram has one right angle, then it is a rectangle. _____

   b. If a quadrilateral is a rectangle, then it is a parallelogram. _____

   c. If a quadrilateral is a kite, then it is a parallelogram. _____

   d. If both sets of opposite sides of a quadrilateral are congruent, then the opposite angles are also congruent. _____

   e. If one pair of opposite sides of a quadrilateral is parallel, the sides are congruent. _____

   f. If a quadrilateral has one right angle, then it is a rectangle. _____

3. Sam and Pete are having an argument about whether every square is a rectangle.
   a. What do you think? Is every square a rectangle?

   b. Explain why or why not.

Lesson 2 Summary Answer Key (Teacher Resource 4)

1. Check all properties that always apply to each shape.

	Opposite Sides Parallel	Four Congruent Sides	Opposite Sides Congruent	Opposite Angles Congruent	Four Congruent Angles	Four Right Angles
Quadrilateral						
Rectangle	✓		✓	✓	✓	✓
Parallelogram	✓		✓	✓		
Square	✓	✓	✓	✓	✓	✓
Rhombus	✓	✓	✓	✓		
Trapezoid						
Kite						
Dart						

2. True or false? If the answer is false, show a counterexample.
   a. If a parallelogram has one right angle, then it is a rectangle. **True**
   b. If a quadrilateral is a rectangle, then it is a parallelogram. **True**
   c. If a quadrilateral is a kite, then it is a parallelogram. **False—A kite is never a parallelogram as its opposite sides cannot be the same length.**
   d. If both sets of opposite sides of a quadrilateral are congruent, then the opposite angles are also congruent. **True**
   e. If one pair of opposite sides of a quadrilateral is parallel, the sides are congruent. **False—Think about a trapezoid.**
   f. If a quadrilateral has one right angle, then it is a rectangle. **False—There are many counterexamples, but here is one:**

3. Sam and Pete are having an argument about whether every square is a rectangle.
   a. What do you think? Is every square a rectangle? **Yes, every square is a rectangle.**
   b. Explain why or why not. **A square has four right angles. Because this satisfies the definition of a rectangle, the square is a rectangle.**

Lesson 3: Areas of Triangles

Instructional Purpose

- To identify the base and height of a triangle.
- To develop and apply a formula for the area of a triangle.
- To find a method for finding the area of a triangle when base and height are not known.

Materials and Handouts

- A 4" x 6" rectangle cut out of 1" grid paper
- Scissors
- 5 x 5 pin geoboards
- What Is the Area? (Handout 3A)
- Geoboard Dot Paper (Handout 3B)
- Area of Triangles (Handout 3C)
- More Areas of Triangles (Handout 3D)

Activities

1. Tell students that in this lesson they will be developing a formula for finding the area of a triangle, but first you need to clarify some terms.

2. Distinguish area from length and emphasize their respective units.
   a. Show a 4" x 6" rectangle that is cut from 1" grid paper. Ask what the length and the width of the rectangle are. What units are used to describe the length and width? Emphasize that they are units in one dimension and can be measured with a ruler (inches in this case).
   b. Shade in the rectangle and tell students that the shaded part is the *area* of the rectangle and is measured by determining how many 1" squares are needed to cover it. Ask what the area of this rectangle is and how they know. Let students share their ideas. Encourage them to use the terms *length* and *width*. Give another rectangle problem and ask them to find the area. Make sure they include square units as part of the answer and that they can explain how they got their answers. Ask for a generalization: *If we know the length and width of a rectangle, how can we use them to find the area?* Nudge students to the formula Area = Length x Width. Emphasize the definition of *area* as the amount of surface of a region or shape (measured in square units).

3. Discuss base and height/altitude.
   a. Show a triangle and ask students what they think the term *base* of the triangle might mean. Help them to clarify their ideas so that they understand that each of the three sides can be a base, but you will choose to place the side you are using as the base so it is parallel to the floor. Emphasize the definition of the *base of a triangle* as one of the three sides of the triangle, usually the one at the bottom that is parallel to the floor.
   b. Ask what you might mean by the term *height* of the triangle (which is the same as the term *altitude* in geometry). Nudge them to understand that it is the perpendicular distance from the vertex opposite the base to the line

containing the base. Use a few examples of different types of triangles and ask students to identify the base and height as you rotate the triangle onto each of its three bases. Include triangles that are right and obtuse.

4. Tell students that we now know how to find the area of a rectangle, but the big question of this lesson is: *How do we find the area of a triangle?* Cut the 4" x 6" rectangle along a diagonal to form two right triangles. Ask: *What is the area of one of these triangles?* Have students suggest ideas. Identify the base and height of the triangle and note that they were called length and width in the rectangle. Students should conclude that the triangle has half the area of the corresponding rectangle.

5. Have students complete **What Is the Area? (Handout 3A)** and discuss in groups and as a whole class.

6. Give each student a 5 x 5 pin geoboard. If you do not have a classroom set of geoboards, you may copy the page labeled **Geoboard Dot Paper (Handout 3B)** at the end of this lesson. Have students copy the triangles below as you show them. For each one, ask students to identify the length of the base and height. Then they should find the area of the triangle and explain how they determined their answers. Collect the data on paper or on the board. Lead a discussion using questions such as *What patterns do you see?* and *Can you find a general method to find the area of any triangle?* Students should converge on a formula that says the area of a triangle is equal to half the base times the height.

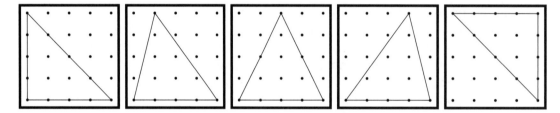

7. Have students copy the following triangle onto their geoboards and test their new formula to find the area of the triangle. They should verify by another method of reasoning. (Note that the base is now vertical. Students may turn their geoboards to see that.) Share results.

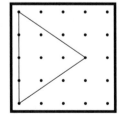

8. Use geoboards to have students form a triangle that looks like the triangle in Figure 3.1 (obtuse triangle with base 2 and height 4). Ask whether this triangle follows the triangle area rule you have made. Have them work in groups to find the area. Share their ideas. (Yes, the formula A = 1/2 x base x height works here. They can find the area of a larger right triangle and cut off the smaller right triangle that they don't need, as demonstrated in Figure 3.1.)

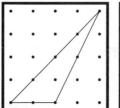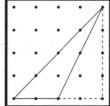

Figure 3.1. Finding the area of a triangle by subtracting from a larger right triangle.

9. Have students complete the first two items in **Area of Triangles (Handout 3C)** and discuss as a group. Then have them look at the third triangle and ask if the area formula will work on this one. (They should notice that we cannot determine the base and height of the triangle by counting units on the geoboard. In the future, when they learn the Pythagorean Theorem, they will be able to find those lengths, but for today they will have to find another method.) Have them work individually and then in groups on the last item on the handout. Discuss as a whole class. It is likely that they will use the method of finding the area in which you enclose the triangle with a rectangle, find the area of the shaded right triangles, and subtract those areas from the area of the rectangle, as shown in Figure 3.2. If they need a hint, show them a geoboard with the outline of a rectangle around the triangle and see if they can figure it out from there.

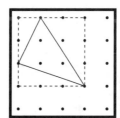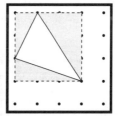

Figure 3.2. Finding the area of a triangle by subtracting from a rectangle.

10. Have students complete **More Areas of Triangles (Handout 3D)** for further practice.

Assessment

- Observations (group and class discussions)
- Areas of Triangles (Handout 3C)
- More Areas of Triangles (Handout 3D)

Notes to Teacher

- An obtuse triangle that is oriented as in Figure 3.3 can confuse students when finding the altitude because the altitude is outside the triangle. You may suggest that it is similar to finding the altitude or height of a mountain by dropping a rope from the highest "peak" with a weight attached. The length of that rope is the height.

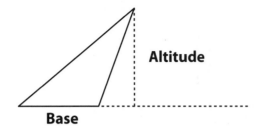

Figure 3.3. Finding the height of an obtuse triangle.

- You may use the symbol that mathematicians use for labeling right angles on diagrams. It is a tiny square. Figure 3.4 is an example.

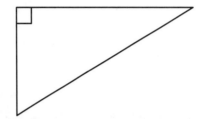

Figure 3.4. Indication of a right angle.

- If students have not used a geoboard before, make sure they know that 1 unit is the distance between two pegs. So the distance between five horizontal pegs is 4 units. Note that the diagonal distance between two pegs is longer than 1 unit, as illustrated in Figure 3.5.

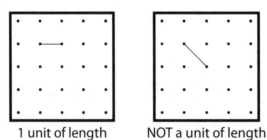

1 unit of length   NOT a unit of length

Figure 3.5. Measuring units of length on a geoboard.

Extensions

- Have students use a 5 x 5 pin geoboard to make as many different triangles of area 6 square units as they can. Have them copy their results onto copies of Geoboard Dot Paper (Handout 3B). (If the classroom does not have geoboards, students can do all work on Handout 3B.) Make sure that students label the lengths of the sides of each triangle.
- There is a theorem (a statement that has been proven to be true for all cases) called Pick's Theorem that applies to triangles constructed on a geoboard. It says: *Let B = the number of dots on the boundary of the triangle, and let I = the number of dots in the interior of the triangle. A = I + 1/2 B – 1.* We are not in a position to prove it here, but have students make some triangles on geoboards or on Geoboard Dot Paper (Handout 3B), then find their areas using both Pick's formula and the A = 1/2 x b x h formula. They should be the same.

- Have students complete the following journal writing assignment: Both Jan and Karl can find the area of a triangle accurately, but they do it differently. Jan knows a formula: 1/2 base times height. Karl draws a rectangle around the triangle, finds the area of the rectangle, and then takes half of that area. What are the advantages and disadvantages of each method? Which one do you prefer?

Name: _____ Date: _____

What Is the Area? (Handout 3A)

Directions: Answer the questions for each triangle. Be sure to explain how you found the area.

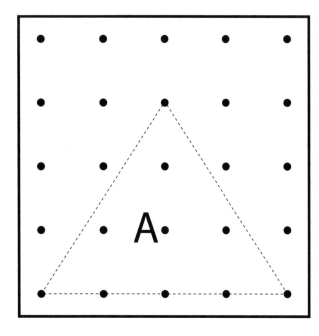

Triangle A:

Length of base:_____

Altitude/height:_____

Area:_____

How did you find the area?

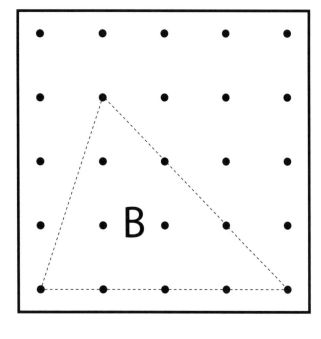

Triangle B:

Length of base:_____

Altitude/height:_____

Area:_____

How did you find the area?

What Is the Area? Answer Key
(Teacher Resource 1)

Directions: Answer the questions for each triangle. Be sure to explain how you found the area.

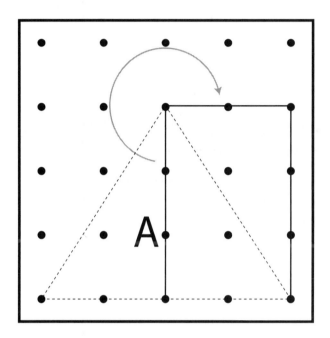

Triangle A:

Length of base: **4 units**

Altitude/height: **3 units**

Area: **6 square units**

How did you find the area?
Answers will vary. Here is one example: Draw the height to form two right triangles. Rotate the left triangle to form a 2 x 3 rectangle. A = 2 x 3 = 6 square units.

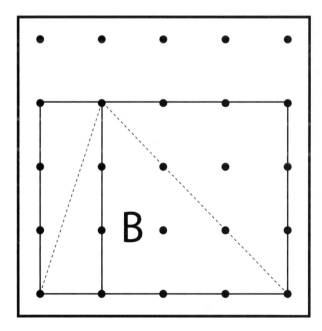

Triangle B:

Length of base: **4 units**

Altitude/height: **3 units**

Area: **6 square units**

How did you find the area?
Answers will vary. Here is one example: Draw a 4 x 3 rectangle around the triangle as shown. Divide it into two rectangles as shown (1 x 3 and 3 x 3). Each of the resulting right triangles is half the area of one of the rectangles, so their areas are 1.5 and 4.5. The sum of these is 6 square units.

Name: _____ Date: _____

Geoboard Dot Paper (Handout 3B)

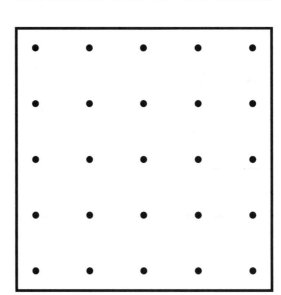

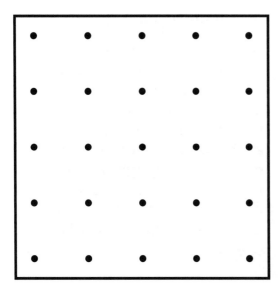

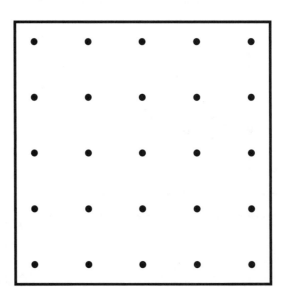

Name: _____ Date: _____

Area of Triangles (Handout 3C)

Directions: If the smallest square is one unit of area, find the area of each triangle. Explain your reasoning.

1.

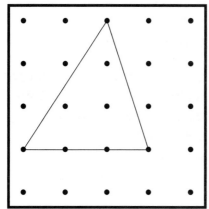

Area: _____

Explanation:

2.

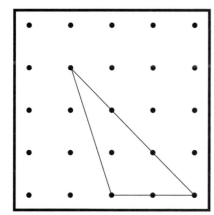

Area: _____

Explanation:

3. This one is a challenge! No side of the triangle is horizontal or vertical. See if you can find the area.

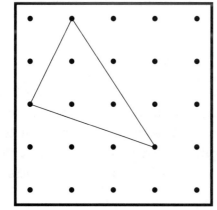

Area: _____

Explanation:

Area of Triangles Answer Key
(Teacher Resource 2)

Directions: If the smallest square is one unit of area, find the area of each triangle. Explain your reasoning.

1.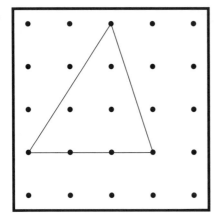

Area: **4.5 square units**

Explanation: **Using the formula for area of a triangle (A = 1/2 x base x height) where base = 3 and height = 3, A = 1/2 x 3 x 3 = 1/2 x 9 = 4.5 square units.**

2.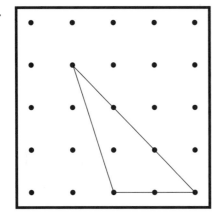

Area: **3 square units**

Explanation: **Using the same formula with base = 2 and height = 3, A = 1/2 x base x height = 1/2 x 2 x 3 = 1/2 x 6 = 3 square units.**

3. This one is a challenge! No side of the triangle is horizontal or vertical. See if you can find the area.

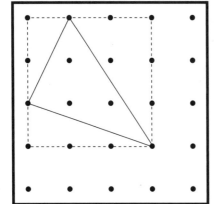

Area: **3.5 square units**

Explanation: **Draw a 3 x 3 square of area 9 around the triangle as shown. Find the areas of the three triangles outside the original triangle and subtract them from 9. A = 9 – 1 – 1.5 – 3 = 3.5 square units.**

More Areas of Triangles (Handout 3D)

1. Use the triangle at the right to answer these two questions:
   a. Give the measure of the base and height of this triangle.

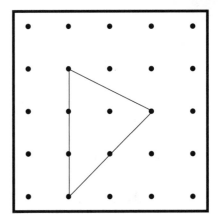

   b. Find the area of the triangle. Show how you know.

2. Find the area of this triangle. Show how you know.

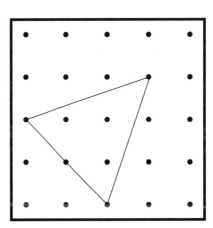

1. Use the triangle at the right to answer these two questions:

   a. Give the measure of the base and height of this triangle.

      Base = 3 units, height = 2 units

   b. Find the area of the triangle. Show how you know.

      Area = 1/2 x base x height = 1/2 x 3 x 2 = 3 sq. units

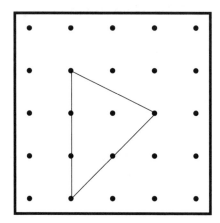

2. Find the area of this triangle. Show how you know.

   The area is 4 square units. The easiest way to determine the area is to circumscribe a 3 x 3 square around the triangle, then subtract the areas of the three right triangles that are outside the triangle.

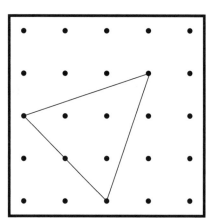

Lesson 4: Areas of Parallelograms and Kites

Instructional Purpose

- To develop, understand, and use strategies to find the areas of parallelograms and kites.

Materials and Handouts

- Scissors
- A 4" x 6" card for each student
- Two sheets of rectangular paper for each student
- Rulers
- Area of Triangles and Rectangles (Handout 4A)
- Area of Parallelograms and Kites (Handout 4B)
- More Practice (Handout 4C)

Activities

1. Review the concepts of area of a rectangle as length times width and area of a triangle as half the base times height. Use **Area of Triangles and Rectangles (Handout 4A)** to do this. Note that area is given in *square* units (which emphasizes that it is telling how many squares of a certain size are needed to cover the shape). Tell students that they will use this information to find the area of some other quadrilaterals in this lesson.

2. Ask students to recall the definition of a parallelogram. Distribute 4" x 6" cards to students. Either have them marked to be cut into a parallelogram or ask students how the card could be made into a parallelogram. After each student has cut the card to make a parallelogram, distribute **Area of Parallelograms and Kites (Handout 4B)** and ask them to look at the first problem. They should use the parallelogram made from the card to answer the question. Discuss in groups and then as a whole class. There are several ways to find the area and students should share what they find. Make sure they see that by cutting off a right triangle on the left and sliding it to the right, they make a rectangle with the same area as the parallelogram. They should arrive at the conclusion that the area of a parallelogram is the same as the area of a rectangle with length and width equal to the base and height of the parallelogram.

3. Review the definition of a rhombus. Have students make one with a rectangular piece of paper and scissors as follows:
   - Fold the paper into quarters.
   - Mark a point 3 inches along one of the folded sides. Mark a point 2 inches along the other folded side.
   - Cut along a line that connects the two marks (from one folded side to the other).
   - Unfold the quadrilateral. You will have a shape as illustrated in Figure 4.1. It will have four congruent sides and therefore is a rhombus. Note that the diagonals of the rhombus intersect at right angles and bisect each other. Ask the students if they can see why.

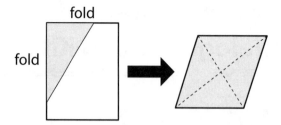

Figure 4.1. Making a rhombus.

Ask students to investigate a way to find the area of the rhombus. They may cut it apart and move the pieces if they wish. Debrief their methods in a whole group discussion. Then have them do the second problem in Handout 4B.

4. Review the definition of a kite. Students should make one with a rectangular piece of paper and scissors as follows:
    *   Fold a rectangular piece of paper in half.
    *   Use the fold as one side of a scalene triangle and draw two other sides that are not the same length.
    *   Cut along the two new sides.
    *   Make a crease along the height of the triangle. (Consider the folded side the base.)
    *   Unfold the resulting quadrilateral and it will be a kite, as shown in Figure 4.2.

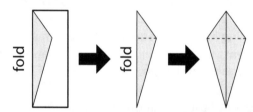

Figure 4.2. Making a kite.

Ask students to investigate a way to find the area of this kite. (You may assign estimated lengths to the diagonals if you want a numerical result, but the main idea is to find that the area can be rearranged into rectangles.) They may cut it apart and move the pieces if they wish. Debrief their methods in a whole-group discussion. Then have them do the third problem in Handout 4B.

5. Ask students if they can describe, in words or in a formula, a general way to find the area of each of these quadrilaterals:
    *   parallelogram
    *   rhombus
    *   kite

The most important thing is for students to develop a strategy for finding each area. If they express that as a formula, that is fine, but a formula is not required. There are formulas included in **Information for Teachers (Teacher Resource 3)** for reference if you need them.

6. Have students complete **More Practice (Handout 4C)** for practice.

Assessment

- Observations (class discussions, group work)
- Area of Parallelograms and Kites (Handout 4B)
- Finding Areas (Handout 4C)
- Journal writing assignment (see Extensions)

Notes to Teacher

- The discovery of a method for finding the area of various polygons is the main value of this lesson. Students are welcome to assign meaningful variables to the lengths in the figures and develop formulas, but they need not write formulas. Memorizing formulas has historically been a popular strategy that teachers promote, but it is not a particularly effective one over time. If students create their own meaningful script of what it means to find the area of each shape, it will serve them well in later years when they need the information. The development of a formula comes naturally to students who see the pattern and want to make the transition from a concrete or pictorial representation to an abstract formula.
- Information for Teachers (Teacher Resource 3) contains more information than is needed in this lesson. You will need it for reference in later lessons.

Extensions

- On the board, draw a square inscribed in an 8" x 8" square as shown below. (The vertices of the inside square rest on the midpoints of the sides of the original square.) Have students copy it into their math journals. Ask them to find the area of the shaded square in as many ways as possible and describe them in their math journals. (32 square inches) There are several different ways to show this. Press your students to show as many as they can.

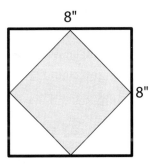

- Have students complete the following journal writing assignment: Sami says you don't need a formula for finding the area of a rhombus because he knows a formula for finding the area of a parallelogram. Do you think his approach is correct? Explain.

Name: _____ Date: _____

Area of Triangles and Rectangles (Handout 4A)

Directions: Find the area of each quadrilateral or triangle. Explain your reasoning.

1.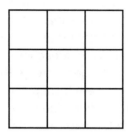

Area: _____

Explanation:

2.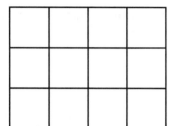

Area: _____

Explanation:

3.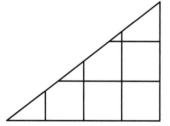

Area: _____

Explanation:

4.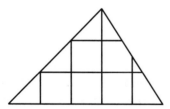

Area: _____

Explanation:

5.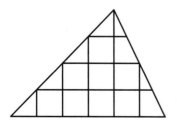

Area: _____

Explanation:

Area of Triangles and Rectangles
Answer Key (Teacher Resource 1)

Directions: Find the area of each quadrilateral or triangle. Explain your reasoning.

1.

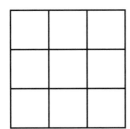

Area: **9 square units**

Explanation: **Area of a rectangle = length x width = 3 x 3 = 9**

2.

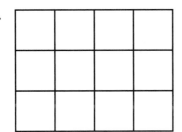

Area: **12 square units**

Explanation: **Area of a rectangle = length x width = 4 x 3 = 12**

3.

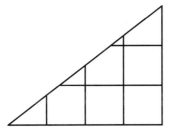

Area: **6 square units**

Explanation: **Area of a triangle = 1/2 x base x height = 1/2 x 4 x 3 = 6**

4.

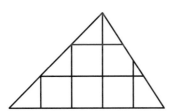

Area: **7.5 square units**

Explanation: **Area of a triangle = 1/2 x base x height = 1/2 x 5 x 3 = 7.5**

5.

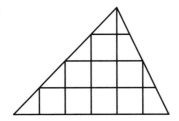

Area: **12 square units**

Explanation: **Area of a triangle = 1/2 x base x height = 1/2 x 6 x 4 = 12**

Area of Parallelograms and Kites (Handout 4B)

Sharon does not like to memorize formulas. She knows how to find the area of a rectangle. So she tries to cut up new geometric shapes and rearrange the pieces into a rectangle so she can find the area. Trace or draw these figures onto another piece of paper. Then cut apart each shape and reassemble it to make a rectangle. Use this technique to find the area of each shape.

1. Parallelogram

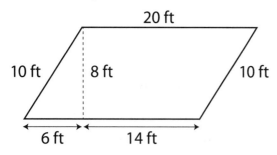

2. Rhombus

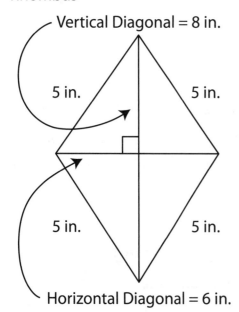

3. Kite

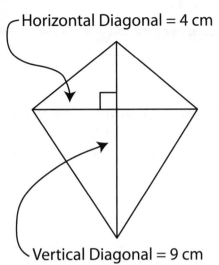

Horizontal Diagonal = 4 cm

Vertical Diagonal = 9 cm

Area of Parallelograms and Kites
Answer Key (Teacher Resource 2)

Sharon does not like to memorize formulas. She knows how to find the area of a rectangle. So she tries to cut up new geometric shapes and rearrange the pieces into a rectangle so she can find the area. Trace or draw these figures onto another piece of paper. Then cut apart each shape and reassemble it to make a rectangle. Use this technique to find the area of each shape.

1. Parallelogram

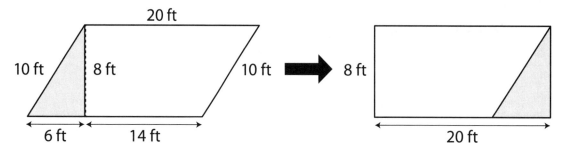

The area of the parallelogram is 160 square ft. You can use two triangles of 24 sq. ft plus a rectangle of 112 sq. ft, or move the triangle from the left to the right and you have a rectangle of 20 ft length and 8 ft width; 20 x 8 = 160.

2. Rhombus

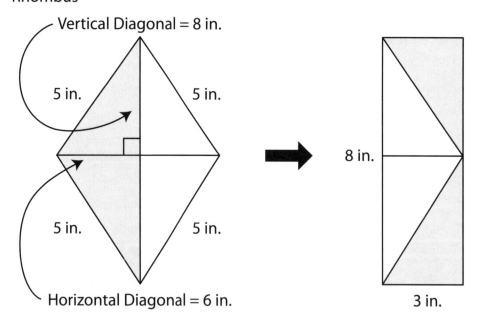

The area of the rhombus is 24 square in. (Note that the diagonals bisect each other.) You may use
- **four triangles with areas of 6 sq. in. each,**
- **two triangles with base 6 in. and height 4 in.,**
- **two triangles with base 8 in. and height 3 in., or**
- **a 3 in. x 8 in. rectangle, as shown above.**

3. Kite

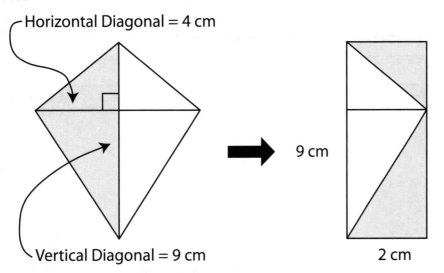

Horizontal Diagonal = 4 cm

Vertical Diagonal = 9 cm

9 cm

2 cm

The area of the kite is 18 square cm. Move the left half to the right and form a rectangle that is 2 cm by 9 cm; 2 x 9 = 18.

© Prufrock Press Inc. • *Polygons Galore!*

This page may be photocopied or reproduced with permission for single classroom use only.

65

Quadrilateral	Formula	Rationale	Example
square	$A = s^2$	Because the length and width of a square are always the same, the formula shows that you have sides that are equal. You can multiply two sides to get the area of the square. This is the same as squaring the sides.	$s = 3$ yd $s^2 = 3$ yd x 3 yd $A = s^2 = 9$ yd^2
rectangle	$A = l \times w$	Because the length and the width of a rectangle are different, the formula must reflect the different sides. To get the area of a rectangle, you multiply the length by the width.	$w = 6$ in. $l = 14$ in. $A = l \times w$ $A = 14$ in. x 6 in. $A = 84$ in.^{2}
parallelogram	$A = b \times h$	As a parallelogram is a quadrilateral with opposite sides that are parallel, you can transform it into a rectangle by cutting the parallelogram along its height and moving the triangle to its opposite end. The length and width of the rectangle are equal to the base and height of the parallelogram.	$h = 6$ cm $b = 17$ cm $A = b \times h$ $A = 17$ cm x 6 cm $A = 102$ cm^2
trapezoid	$A = 1/2 \times h \times (b_1 + b_2)$	A trapezoid is a quadrilateral with two bases of different lengths. By taking the top base of the trapezoid and adding it to the bottom base, a parallelogram can be created with height that is half the height of the trapezoid and a base that is the sum of b_1 and b_2. As the area of a parallelogram is equal to base x height, the area of the trapezoid equals half its height multiplied by the sum of its two bases.	$b_2 = 8$ in. $h = 4$ $b_1 = 12$ in. $A = 1/2 \times h \times (b_1 + b_2)$ $A = 1/2 \times 4$ in. x (12 in. + 8 in.) $A = 1/2 \times 4$ in. x 20 in. $A = 40$ in.^{2}

Quadrilateral	Formula	Rationale	Example
rhombus	$A = 1/2 \times (d_1 \times d_2)$ (where d_1 and d_2 are the length of the diagonals)	A rhombus has four equal sides and its diagonals bisect each other at right angles. If you cut the rhombus up and reassemble it into a rectangle, you can find the area easily; or find the area of one of the triangles and multiply by 4.	$d_2 = 8$ cm, $d_1 = 6$ cm $A = 1/2 \times (d_1 \times d_2)$ $A = 1/2 \times (6 \text{ cm} \times 8 \text{ cm})$ $A = 1/2 \times (48 \text{ cm}^2)$ $A = 24 \text{ cm}^2$
kite	$A = 1/2 \times (d_1 \times d_2)$	If you cut the kite on its longer diagonal, you can move the two triangles on the left to the right and form a rectangle whose area is half the short diagonal times the long diagonal; or you can find the areas of the four right triangles and add them.	$d_2 = 14$ cm, $d_1 = 8$ cm $A = 1/2 \times (d_1 \times d_2)$ $A = 1/2 \times (8 \text{ cm} \times 14 \text{ cm})$ $A = 1/2 \times (112 \text{ cm}^2)$ $A = 56 \text{ cm}^2$

Name: _____ Date: _____

More Practice (Handout 4C)

Directions: Find the area of each quadrilateral. Show how you know.

1. Parallelogram

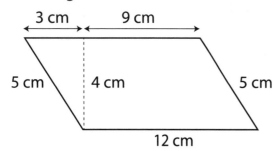

2. Rhombus
   All sides measure 10 yards. The vertical diagonal measures 12 yards. The horizontal diagonal measures 16 yards.

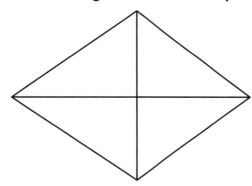

3. Kite

Horizontal Diagonal = 5 ft

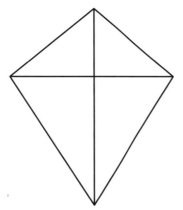

Vertical Diagonal = 12 ft

More Practice Answer Key
(Teacher Resource 4)

Directions: Find the area of each quadrilateral. Show how you know.

1. Parallelogram

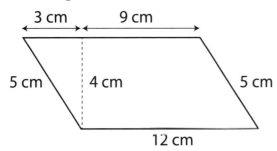

The area of the parallelogram is 48 square cm. If you move the triangle from the left to the right you will have a rectangle of 12 cm length and 4 cm width, and 12 x 4 = 48.

2. Rhombus
   All sides measure 10 yards. The vertical diagonal measures 12 yards. The horizontal diagonal measures 16 yards.

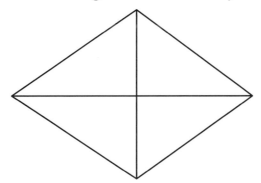

The area of the rhombus is 96 square yd. You may use
- **four triangles with areas of 24 sq. yd each,**
- **two triangles with base 16 yd and height 6 yd,**
- **two triangles with base 12 yd and height 8 yd,**
- **a 12 yd x 8 yd rectangle, or**
- **a 16 yd x 6 yd rectangle.**

3. Kite

Horizontal Diagonal = 5 ft

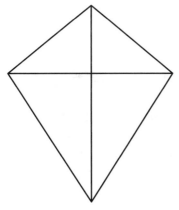

The area of the kite is 30 square ft. Move the left half to the right and form a rectangle that is 2.5 ft by 12 ft; 2.5 x 12 = 30.

Vertical Diagonal = 12 ft

Lesson 5: Areas of Trapezoids

Instructional Purpose

- To develop methods for finding the area of a trapezoid.

Materials and Handouts

- Colored pencils, crayons (optional)
- Scissors
- 4" x 6" notecards (about 10 for each student)
- Area of Trapezoids (Handout 5A)
- Vocabulary Word Study (Handout 5B)

Activities

1. Review the concept of area of these quadrilaterals:
   - rectangle
   - square
   - parallelogram
   - rhombus

2. Tell students that in this lesson they are going to develop a way to find the area of another quadrilateral: the trapezoid. Have students give examples of trapezoids and the definition from Lesson 2. Discuss the terms *base* and *height* as they apply to trapezoids. There are two bases that are parallel to each other. They are often labeled b_1 and b_2. The height or altitude is the distance between them. (Note that *distance* implies the length of a segment that is perpendicular to both bases.)

3. Give out three 4" x 6" cards to each student. They will create three different trapezoids. Challenge them to perform the following.
   a. Make one cut on a card to create a trapezoid. Label the bases and the height. (It should look as in Figure 5.1 and will have two right angles.)

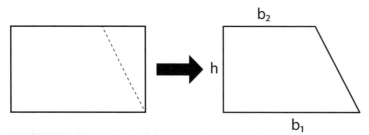

Figure 5.1. Making a trapezoid.

   b. Make an isosceles trapezoid by making two cuts (isosceles implies that the angles at the bases are congruent; the nonparallel sides will also be congruent). Label the bases and the height. Figure 5.2 is an example.

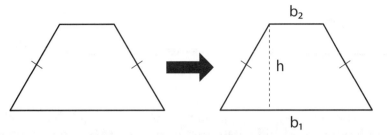

Figure 5.2. An isosceles trapezoid.

    c. Make a third trapezoid by making two cuts so that the nonparallel legs are not congruent. Label the bases and the height. Figure 5.3 is an example.

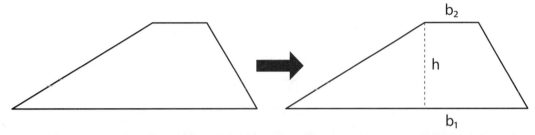

Figure 5.3. Making a trapezoid with noncongruent sides.

    Discuss why all three of these meet the requirements for being labeled a trapezoid. Make sure students reference the definition.

4. Have students use these cards as aids to solving the problems on **Area of Trapezoids (Handout 5A).** They should transfer the measurements on the worksheet to their cards. Ask students to work in groups to find the area of the first trapezoid by decomposing (cutting apart) and recomposing parts to make a shape whose area they know how to find. They may use colored pencils to shade areas that need labeling. Debrief results, pressing students for all different ways that might have been used to find the area. (The area is 26 sq. cm.) Have students mark the diagram on the worksheet and write an explanation of how they found the area next to the trapezoid on the worksheet.

5. Have students do the other two problems in groups and discuss their results. Encourage them to use the trapezoids made with the cards, scissors, and colored pencils to demonstrate their thinking. Encourage groups to share all of the ways they thought of to find the answers. (#2 is 156 sq. ft and #3 is 19.5 sq. cm)

6. Ask students to work in groups to describe, in words or in a formula, a general way to find the area of a trapezoid if they know the measurements of the two bases and the height. If they are having trouble, suggest the following.
    • Cut out any trapezoid on a 4" x 6" card or piece of paper. Fold on the midline (called the median) by folding the top base onto the bottom base. Cut along the midline. Rotate the top part as shown so that it joins the lower part forming a parallelogram. Students should determine the measurements of the new parallelogram in terms of base and height. This gives a general formula. Encourage students to develop and state a formula on their own and then debrief. They should give their methods in both words and symbols.

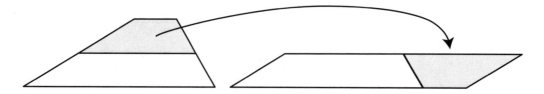

The new polygon is a parallelogram with height that is half the height of the trapezoid and a base that is the sum of b_1 and b_2. Students should use this information to realize that the area of a trapezoid is equal to half its height multiplied by the sum of its two bases.

- Give this problem to try out the formula. Check by decomposing the area into a rectangle and two triangles. This is an isosceles trapezoid.

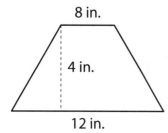

8 in.

4 in.

12 in.

$A = 1/2 \times h \times (b_1 + b_2)$

$A = 1/2 \times 4 \times (12 + 8)$

$A = 40$ sq. in.

7. Have students draw a trapezoid on the front of a card or piece of paper, labeling measurements of all sides and the height, making sure to include units. On the back side, have them show how to find the area. Then have students trade cards and work the problem that was written on the front. When they are finished, they can check the back of the card for the solution.

Assessment

- Observations (class discussions, group work)
- Area of Trapezoids (Handout 5A)
- Journal writing assignment (see Extensions)

Extensions

- Have students complete a **Vocabulary Word Study (Handout 5B)** for the word *trapezoid*.
- Instruct students to look for examples of trapezoids in their school and their community. Have them share their findings with the class.
- Have students complete the following journal writing assignment: Mr. Anderson needs to plant new grass in the trapezoidal park that is shown below. He needs to find the area of the park so that he can buy the right amount of grass seed. What is the area of the park? Explain how you found out. (The area is 1,032 square yd.)

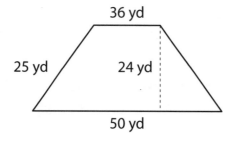

36 yd

25 yd   24 yd

50 yd

Notes to Teacher

- Encourage the terms *decomposing* to indicate the subdividing of geometric shapes and *recomposing* to indicate the rearrangement when the parts are put back together.
- You may find examples of trapezoids in keystones, a popular feature in window architecture. Using the term "concrete keystone," search the Internet for an example to show your students.

Area of Trapezoids (Handout 5A)

Directions: Find the area of each trapezoid. Explain your reasoning.

1.

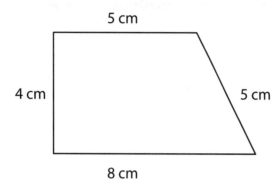

5 cm

4 cm   5 cm

8 cm

Area: _____

Explanation:

2.

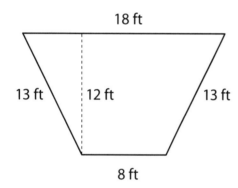

18 ft

13 ft   12 ft   13 ft

8 ft

Area: _____

Explanation:

3.

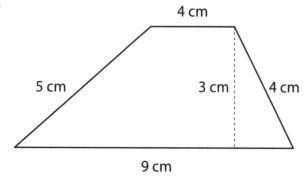

4 cm

5 cm   3 cm   4 cm

9 cm

Area: _____

Explanation:

Area of Trapezoids Answer Key (Teacher Resource 1)

Directions: Find the area of each trapezoid. Explain your reasoning.

1.

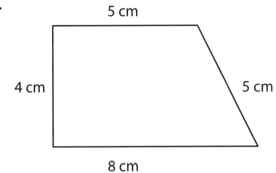

Area: **26 sq. cm**

Explanation:

$A = 1/2 \times h \times (b_1 + b_2)$

$A = 1/2 \times 4 \times (8 + 5)$

$A = 26$

2.

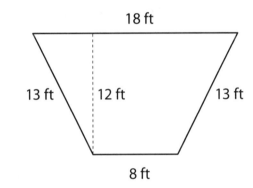

Area: **156 sq. ft**

Explanation:

$A = 1/2 \times h \times (b_1 + b_2)$

$A = 1/2 \times 12 \times (8 + 18)$

$A = 156$

3.

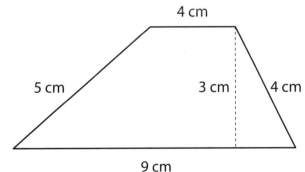

Area: **19.5 sq. cm**

Explanation:

$A = 1/2 \times h \times (b_1 + b_2)$

$A = 1/2 \times 3 \times (9 + 4)$

$A = 19.5$

Name: _____ Date: _____

Vocabulary Word Study (Handout 5B)

Term

Definition	Draw a Picture or Diagram

Real-World Example	Analyze the Word
	Language of origin: **Stems (parts of the word) and what they mean:** **Word families (other words with the same stem[s]):**

Lesson 6: Perimeter vs. Area in Rectangles

Instructional Purpose

- To investigate possible relationships between area and perimeter in rectangles.

Materials and Handouts

- Geoboards
- 38 one-inch cubes per group
- Grid Paper (Handout 6); 2 sheets per group
- Index cards or small pieces of paper, to be used for exit card questions

Activities

1. Introduce the lesson by telling students that you are going to focus on another aspect of rectangles: perimeter. Your main goal is to investigate possible relationships between area and perimeter. Before you start, make sure that everyone understands the idea of perimeter. Define the perimeter of a polygon as the distance around the outside of the polygon. Have students copy a few examples of rectangles that you show them and ask them to find the perimeter, emphasizing that the units are linear (i.e., not squared). Ask for different ways that students figured out their answers. Some may add the four sides, some may double the length and width and add them together, and some may add the length and width and then double the sum. All are valid. Review the idea of perimeter and area. Have students find the perimeter and area of a given rectangle to review.

2. Offer this question for investigation: *Suppose you make different rectangles with the same perimeter. What happens to the area of the rectangle?* Have students work in groups to make suggestions about how they could investigate the question. Ask them to share some ideas.

3. The next activity involves group investigation and data recording. Tell students that you have some materials that might help. Give each group 38 one-inch cubes and a copy of **Grid Paper (Handout 6)**. Tell students to use the cubes to create as many rectangles that have a perimeter of 24 inches as they can. They should use the grid paper to draw all rectangles and label the side lengths. (Note: They need not record rectangles that are rotations of others that are already recorded.) Emphasize that the perimeter of 24 inches is a fixed variable in the experiment as it does not change. Tell students to think about how the changes in length and width affect the area of the rectangle.

4. Debrief the investigation by making a class data table on the board or chart paper. As students offer rectangle data, you might strategically place it in the table so that your end result looks something like the table on page 78:

Width	Length	Perimeter	Area
1 in.	11 in.	24 in.	11 sq. in.
2 in.	10 in.	24 in.	20 sq. in.
3 in.	9 in.	24 in.	27 sq. in.
4 in.	8 in.	24 in.	32 sq. in.
5 in.	7 in.	24 in.	35 sq. in.
6 in.	6 in.	24 in.	36 sq. in.

Ask the students questions such as these:
- What patterns do you notice? (Answers will vary.)
- What is the largest area we can find if the perimeter is 24? (36 square in.) What shape is this? (A square, which is a special kind of rectangle.)
- Do rectangles of the same perimeter have the same area? (No, as shown by the data in the table. The closer the length and width are to each other, the larger the area.)

5. Now offer a different question for investigation: *Suppose you make different rectangles with the same area. What happens to the perimeter?* Have students work in groups to make suggestions about how they could investigate the question. Ask them to share some ideas.

6. Students will likely suggest a procedure for investigating the question by using 24 cubes to make rectangles with an area of 24 square inches (the area is fixed in this investigation). They should work in groups to do this and record all rectangles on grid paper.

7. Debrief student data in a table, as shown below. Groups might want to create their own tables before the whole-class discussion.

Width	Length	Perimeter	Area
1 in.	24 in.	50 in.	24 sq. in.
2 in.	12 in.	28 in.	24 sq. in.
3 in.	8 in.	22 in.	24 sq. in.
4 in.	6 in.	20 in.	24 sq. in.

Ask the students questions such as these:
- What patterns do you notice? (Answers will vary.)
- Review the research question for discussion: *Suppose you make different rectangles with the same area. What happens to the perimeter?* (The perimeter does not stay the same. The closer the length and width are to each other, the smaller the perimeter.)

8. Have students complete these questions on a card or small piece of paper as an exit card:
   a. Find the area and perimeter of a rectangle that measures 8" x 10".
   b. Grace is designing a rectangular brownie pan for people who like edge pieces. Should she make a long skinny pan or a square pan? Explain your reasoning based on the investigations we did today.

Assessment

- Observations (class discussions, group work)
- Exit card questions (see Step 8)
- Journal writing assignment (see Extensions)

Extensions

- Have students choose one of the following questions and design a way to investigate the answer. Instruct them to write about their strategies, their data, and their conclusions.
  - o Suppose you double the length of the rectangle. How is the area affected?
  - o Suppose you double both the length and the width of a rectangle. How is the area affected?
  - o Suppose you double the area of a rectangle. How is the perimeter affected?

- Have students complete the following journal writing assignment: Waldo shows you the following example and says, "Look! As the perimeter of the rectangle increases, the area increases." Do you agree? Explain your reasoning.

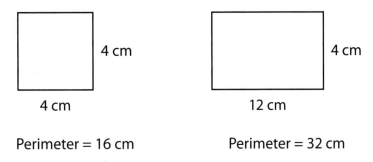

4 cm   4 cm

4 cm   12 cm

Perimeter = 16 cm   Perimeter = 32 cm

Name: _____ Date: _____

Grid Paper (Handout 6)

Lesson 7: Polygon Patterns

Instructional Purpose

- To classify and describe polygons according to their properties.
- To identify, compare, and analyze attributes of polygons.

Materials and Handouts

- Which of These Are Polygons? (Teacher Resource 1) as a page to display on a document camera
- Polygon Patterns (Handout 7A)
- Polygon Patterns (Handout 7A) as a page to display on a document camera
- Vocabulary Word Study (Handout 7B)

Activities

1. Display **Which of These Are Polygons? (Teacher Resource 1)**. You can play a game of "Guess My Rule" in which you say you know the rule for what can be called a polygon and students guess what that rule is after getting feedback from you on their guesses. Focus on the shapes, one at a time, and give feedback on the first few by telling whether it is or is not a polygon. Then pause and ask for student guesses on the rest before you tell them. When you finish, ask them what they think the requirements are for a shape to be called a polygon. They can work in groups and then you can debrief as a whole group.

   Make sure that you eventually converge on the following properties of a polygon:
   - it is a closed figure,
   - it lies in a plane (2-D),
   - it is made of three or more line segments, and
   - its segments do not "cross over" each other (the mathematical term is *simple*—it has no segments that intersect other than at endpoints of the segments).

   You may want to review Teacher Resource 1 with the this list of properties to verify the polygons you identified earlier.

2. Ask students to recall that in earlier lessons they studied both triangles and quadrilaterals. Ask: *Based on what we know now about polygons, are triangles and quadrilaterals polygons?* (Yes)

3. Ask: *What do you think is meant by a "regular" polygon?* Take student suggestions and then go back to Teacher Resource 1. Show students that the only regular polygon on the page is the pentagon (Item N). If they don't suggest the correct meaning of "regular," give another example such as an equilateral triangle. Students should eventually arrive at the idea that a regular polygon is a polygon with all angles congruent and all sides congruent (e.g., a stop sign is a regular octagon). Continue discussion with questions such as:
   - Can you think of a quadrilateral that has four angles of the same measure but sides are not the same length? (A nonsquare rectangle)

- Is this polygon regular? (No, all angles must be congruent and all sides must be congruent.)
- What kind of quadrilateral is regular? (A square)

4. Distribute **Polygon Patterns (Handout 7A)**. Work through the first problem with students by reading the Polygon Description for Number 1 aloud. Draw the appropriate triangle. Ask students if they agree with your selection. If they do, ask students to name the polygon. Write the word *triangle or scalene triangle* in the Polygon Name box.

5. Direct student pairs to work through Number 6 in the same manner. Explain that student pairs must select, justify, and agree upon a name for the polygon before entering it into the appropriate boxes on the Polygon Patterns sheet. Explain that an individual student's sketches may be different from his or her partner's sketches, but that both partners should agree that the sketches are fair representations of the polygon being described.

6. Tell students that polygons with more than four sides take on Greek prefixes to describe the number of angles and sides. Give them a list of Greek prefixes as follows in order to fill out the rest of the handout.
   - penta = 5
   - hexa = 6
   - hepta = 7
   - octa = 8
   - ennea or nona = 9 (Note: *ennea* stems from Greek, whereas the more common *nona* stems from Latin)
   - deca = 10
   - hendeca = 11
   - dodeca = 12

7. Ask students to think of other English words that use these prefixes (e.g., an octopus has eight legs, decade means 10 years, a septuagenarian is a person in his or her 70s). Discuss the connection between the **Vocabulary Word Study (Handout 7B)** "word families" section and the prefixes.

8. Ask: *If you start with a heptagon and take away two angles and two sides, what polygon remains?* (A pentagon) Have students spend several minutes generating such riddles with their partners. Student partners may wish to share riddles with other student pairs or with the whole class. Encourage students to create riddles with different operations.

Assessment
- Observations (class discussions, partner work)
- Polygon Patterns (Handout 7A)

Notes to Teacher
- When we say that a polygon is a "plane" figure or that it "lies in a plane" it means that it is flat. If students are not familiar with the term *plane* in the geometric sense, explain that it is an imaginary flat surface. Therefore, a polygon is flat.

- You may want to use geoboards to have students make polygons. If you use geoboards that have a "circular" side, you can make a regular dodecagon (12-gon) easily.
- The names for polygons that have 13–20 sides are:
  o 13: triskaidecagon or tridecagon
  o 14: tetrakaidecagon or tetradecagon
  o 15: pentakaidecagon or pentadecagon
  o 16: hexakaidecagon or hexadecagon
  o 17: heptakaidecagon or heptadecagon
  o 18: octakaidecagon or octadecagon
  o 19: enneakaidecagon, enneadecagon, or nonadecagon
  o 20: icosagon
    (Note: These names are not standardized, and variations appear in different sources.)

- If a polygon has a large number of sides, it is awkward to use a name. You may name the polygon by the number of sides followed by the prefix "gon." For example, a 19-sided polygon would be a 19-gon.
- Don't forget that any polygon with more than three sides can be either convex or concave.

Extensions

- Cut a strip of paper no more than one inch wide from the long direction of a piece of copy paper. Slowly tie it into an overhand knot and flatten it as it gets tight. Ask students to predict beforehand what the shape will be when flattened (it will be a regular pentagon).
- Have students explore the question: *How many diagonals are there in a given polygon?* Use a table such as the following, where n = the number of sides of the polygon, to scaffold the data.

# sides	# diagonals
3	0
4	2
5	5
6	9
10	35
100	4,850
n	$[n(n-3)] \div 2$

- Ask students to complete a Vocabulary Word Study page for the word *polygon*. Emphasize that the word polygon comes from "many angles" but most people think of the word as meaning a shape with "many sides." (This is true because, when there are many angles, there are also many sides.)

Which of These Are Polygons?
(Teacher Resource 1)

A	**B**	**C**
D	**E**	**F**
G	**H**	**I**
J	**K**	**L**
M	**N**	**O**

Which of These Are Polygons?
Answer Key (Teacher Resource 2)

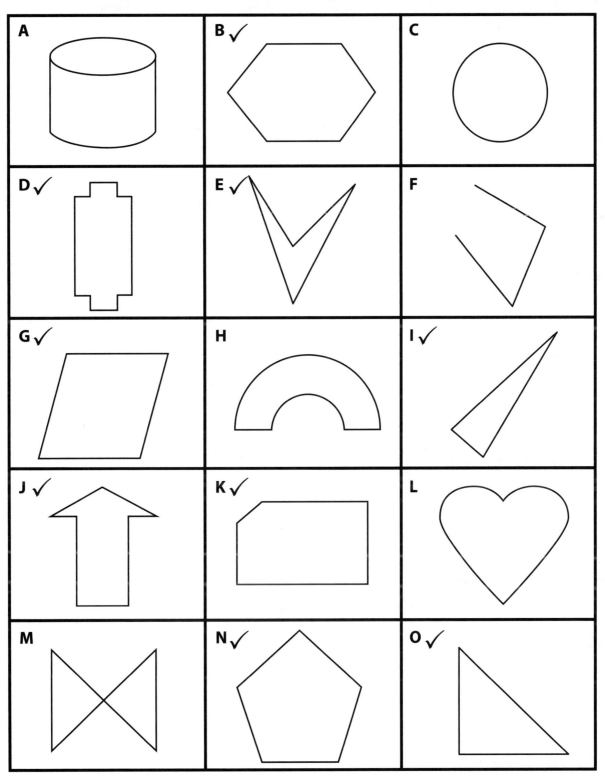

Name: _____ Date: _____

Polygon Patterns (Handout 7A)

Polygon Description	Polygon Name	Sketch
1. A three-sided polygon having three angles of different measures		
2. A four-sided polygon having all right angles		
3. A four sided polygon having equal-length sides meeting at right angles		
4.	parallelogram	
5. A four-sided polygon having four sides of equal length		
6. A four-sided polygon having exactly one pair of parallel sides		
7. A five-sided polygon		
8. A six-sided polygon		
	heptagon	
9. An eight-sided polygon		
10.	nonagon	
11. A 10-sided polygon		
12. A 12-sided polygon		

Polygon Patterns Answer Key
(Teacher Resource 3)

Polygon Description	Polygon Name	Sketch
1. A three-sided polygon having three angles of different measures	**(scalene) triangle**	
2. A four-sided polygon having all right angles	**square or rectangle**	
3. A four sided polygon having equal-length sides meeting at right angles	**square**	
4. **A four-sided polygon with two pairs of parallel sides**	parallelogram	
5. A four-sided polygon having four sides of equal length	**rhombus**	
6. A four-sided polygon having exactly one pair of parallel sides	**trapezoid**	
7. A five-sided polygon	**pentagon**	**(Any polygon with 5 sides)**
8. A six-sided polygon	**hexagon**	**(Any polygon with 6 sides)**
9. **A seven-sided polygon**	heptagon	**(Any polygon with 7 sides)**
10. An eight-sided polygon	**octagon**	**(Any polygon with 8 sides)**
11. **A nine-sided polygon**	nonagon	**(Any polygon with 9 sides)**
12. A 10-sided polygon	**decagon**	**(Any polygon with 10 sides)**
13. A 12-sided polygon	**dodecagon**	**(Any polygon with 12 sides)**

Vocabulary Word Study (Handout 7B)

Term

Definition	Draw a Picture or Diagram

Real-World Example	Analyze the Word
	Language of origin: **Stems (parts of the word) and what they mean:** **Word families (other words with the same stem[s]):**

Lesson 8: The Particulars of Polyhedra

Instructional Purpose

- To distinguish between a polygon and a polyhedron.
- To discover the five Platonic solids.

Materials and Handouts

- Materials to construct polyhedra (see Step 6 for suggestions; Polydrons® are best)
- Cube or rectangular prism (such as a chalk box or cereal box)
- Polyhedron Construction (Handout 8A–1 & 2) copied onto cardstock or other heavy paper
- Platonic Solids (Handout 8B)

Activities

1. Show students a cube or rectangular prism such as a chalk box or cereal box. Ask: Is this a polygon? (No—it does not lie in a plane. It has "faces" that are polygons; so parts of it are polygons, but the whole is not a polygon.) Tell them that it is an example of a polyhedron (plural: polyhedra or polyhedrons).

2. Ask students to consider earlier lessons concerning triangles, quadrilaterals, and polygons. What do they imagine are the similarities and differences between polygons and polyhedra? (Answers will vary but some observations might be: polyhedra are made up of faces that are polygons; polyhedra are three-dimensional figures while polygons are two-dimensional; they both have angles—in a polygon they are formed by line segments while in a polyhedron they are formed where two polygons are joined at an edge; both have vertices.)

3. Have half of the students use **Polyhedron Construction (Handout 8A–1)** to make a polyhedron and the other half use **Polyhedron Construction (Handout 8A–2)** to make a different polyhedron. The patterns on the handout are called *nets*. A net is a two-dimensional pattern that forms a polyhedron when folded into a three-dimensional shape. Students should cut out the net, fold on the dotted lines, and tape together. (The first is a regular tetrahedron: four faces that are all congruent triangles; the second is a triangular prism: two of the faces are congruent triangles, and the other three faces are congruent rectangles.)

4. Compare and contrast the two solids. Both are polyhedra, but one has faces that are all identical (congruent) while the other has faces of two different shapes. Tell students that the first one is called a *tetrahedron*. Ask why they think this name is appropriate. (Tetra means "four" and it has four faces.) Tell them that this particular tetrahedron is a regular polyhedron because all of its faces are congruent regular polygons. The second one is a triangular prism. It is not regular. (Note: The definition of a prism is "a three-dimensional figure with bases that lie in parallel planes, are congruent, and are joined by parallelograms"—in this case, the parallelograms are rectangles.)

5. Distribute **Platonic Solids (Handout 8B).** Explain the terms:
    *   *face*—a polygonal surface of a geometric solid
    *   *edge*—the line where two faces meet
    *   *vertex* (plural: vertices)—a point where the edges meet

    Ask students to count the number of faces, edges, and vertices in the tetrahedron and enter the information in the first row of the handout.

6. Explain to students that their job is to discover which polygons to use to build what mathematicians consider the five regular polyhedra. They know one already: the tetrahedron. Distribute materials and give students time to explore. This may be an open exploration in which they are given no hints or you may package materials such as Polydrons® or polygons cut from cardstock in sandwich bags to guide their construction. The following are the other four regular polyhedra that you want students to discover:
    *   hexahedron (cube), formed by six squares
    *   octahedron, formed by eight equilateral triangles
    *   dodecahedron, formed by 12 pentagons
    *   icosahedron, formed by 20 equilateral triangles

    The following are some suggested materials to help perform this activity:
    *   Polydrons® (these commercially available materials are plastic polygons that can serve as faces and be snapped together or unsnapped easily)
    *   Polygons cut out of old file folders (students can tape them together)
    *   Toothpicks and marshmallows, Play-Doh®, or clay
    *   Commercially available rod and connector sets (e.g., Zometools, K'Nex, Tinkertoys, Magformers)

7. Debrief the findings of your students. They should have discovered four more regular solids for a total of five. These are called the *Platonic solids* as they were known to the ancient Greeks and described by Plato around 350 B.C. Have students rotate each solid and notice that no matter what face it rests on, it should look the same. Ask students to use their knowledge of the Greek prefixes from Lesson 7 to guess what each of these polyhedra might be called. Record the names in the table in Handout 8B. If students haven't already done so, have them count and record the number of edges, faces, and vertices for each figure.

Assessment

*   Observations (class discussions)
*   Completed constructed polyhedra
*   Platonic Solids (Handout 8B)

Notes to Teacher

*   A good resource on Platonic solids is Lesson 4 of Chapter 5 in the book *Mathematics: A Human Endeavor* by Harold Jacobs.

Extensions

*   Introduce the semiregular polyhedra that use two or more different regular polygons as faces to form a solid whose vertices are all surrounded by the

same kinds of polygons in the same (or reverse) order. These are called the Archimedean solids and are named after Archimedes, a Greek mathematician who lived in the 3rd century B.C. There are 13 of them.

- Ask students to find out more about Plato, for whom the Platonic solids are named.

- Have students use the table of data from Handout 8B to look for a relationship pattern between the edges, faces, and vertices. You want them to see that the sum of the number of faces and number of vertices is always two more than the number of edges. Ask students to write a mathematical statement that expresses this pattern. Can they generate more than one way to write it? Is one way more useful than another?

     Here are two ways to express the relationship. If F = the number of faces, V = the number of vertices, and E = the number of edges, then:

$$F + V = E + 2 \text{ or}$$
$$F + V - E = 2$$

     This is often called Euler's Formula for Polyhedra and it was discovered by Leonhard Euler about 1750. Euler (pronounced "oiler") was a very famous Swiss mathematician.

- Have your students find out more about Leonhard Euler. A good resource is the book *Mathematicians Are People, Too*, by Luetta Reimer and Wilbert Reimer.

Name: _____ Date: _____

Polyhedron Construction (Handout 8A–1)

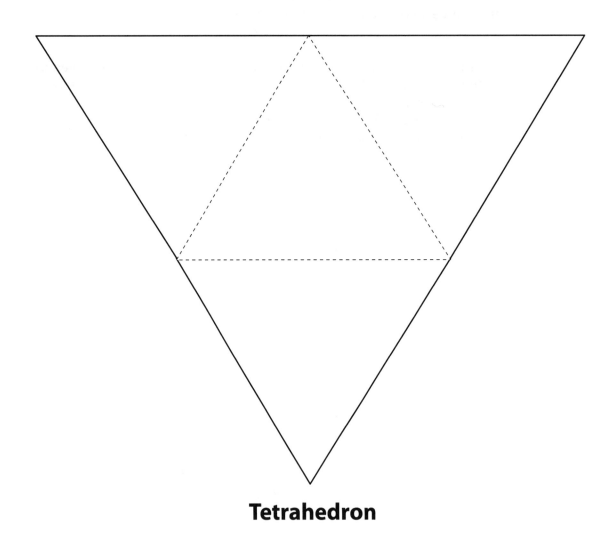

Tetrahedron

Polyhedron Construction (Handout 8A–2)

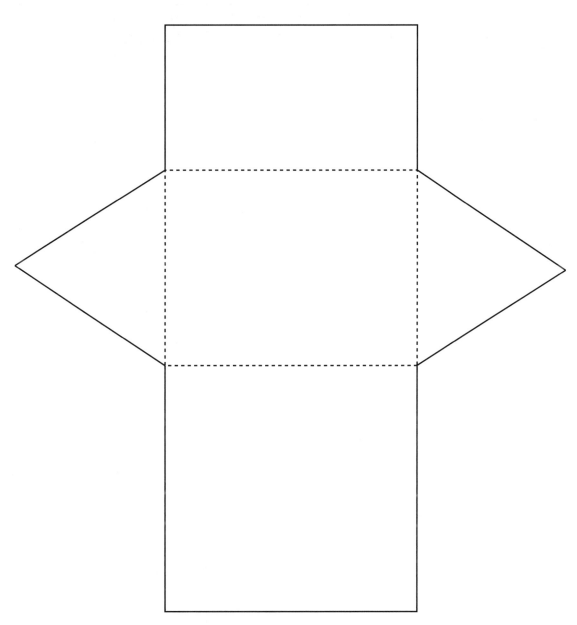

Triangular Prism

Name: _____ Date: _____

Platonic Solids (Handout 8B)

Directions: Use the materials you have been given to discover the five regular polyhedra, otherwise known as Platonic solids. Fill in the information for each.

Platonic Solid	Shape of the Faces	Number of Faces	Number of Vertices	Number of Edges
tetrahedron				

Platonic Solids Answer Key
(Teacher Resource 1)

Directions: Use the materials you have been given to discover the five regular polyhedra, otherwise known as Platonic solids. Fill in the information for each.

Platonic Solid	Shape of the Faces	Number of Faces	Number of Vertices	Number of Edges
tetrahedron	triangles	4	4	6
hexahedron (also known as a cube)	squares	6	8	12
octahedron	triangles	8	6	12
dodecahedron	pentagons	12	20	30
icosahedron	triangles	20	12	30

Lesson 9: Geometry Beyond the Textbook

Instructional Purpose

- To recognize applications of polygons and polyhedra in the real world.

Materials and Handouts

- Access to the Internet, art books, and magazines
- A few collected examples of geometry in the real world
- Patty Paper or some other tracing paper
- Polygons on the Floor (Handout 9A)
- Polygons and Polyhedra Are Everywhere (Handout 9B)

Activities

1. Have students look around the classroom and list all of the examples of polygons and polyhedra they see. Then show or cite some examples, such as snowflakes (which are always hexagonal) or a Toblerone chocolate box (which is a triangular prism). See the Notes to Teacher section for more ideas.

2. Introduce **Polygons on the Floor (Handout 9A),** which has a drawing of a pattern taken from the floor of the Charlotte Douglas International Airport in Charlotte, NC. Have students work individually to find all of the polygons they can in the design. Have students share their polygons by tracing them and posting them to a bulletin board or poster.

3. Students should work in small groups either in class or outside of class to collect examples of polygons and polyhedra in the real world. They should use **Polygons and Polyhedra Are Everywhere (Handout 9B)** to prompt their thinking about different categories of applications. They should try to fill in examples from all of the categories. If they find new categories, they can fill in the bottom row and use the back of the page. Encourage students to take photos with a digital camera if they can.

4. Have groups share their findings. Prompt some discussion with questions such as:
   - *What games use polygons?* Tell students to consider the courts, fields, and tables of sports such as basketball, football, baseball, billiards, tennis, and ping-pong.
   - *Why do you think triangles are used in the construction of bridges?* (The triangle is the most stable polygon; you can verify this by making polygons with tongue depressors that are connected with brass paper fasteners through holes punched in the tongue depressors. The sides of the triangle will not move once they are joined, whereas the sides of a rectangle or any other polygon will.)
   - *What is the most common polygon you found? What is the most common polyhedron you found?*

Assessment

- Observations (class discussions, group work)
- Polygons on the Floor (Handout 9A)
- Polygons and Polyhedra Are Everywhere (Handout 9B)

Notes to Teacher

- More sources of real-world polygons that can be brought into the classroom include:
  - real estate ads;
  - brochures from tile stores;
  - pictures of bridges;
  - pictures of the Parthenon, the Washington Monument, and the Pentagon;
  - checkerboards;
  - hexagonal honeycombs of a bee's nest;
  - crystals in geological formations; and
  - logos of car companies such as Chrysler or Mitsubishi.

- You might make a bulletin board display of the examples that students find. Invite them to add to the board over the course of the next few weeks.
- The unit Postassessment follows this lesson and should be administered when the unit is complete.

Extensions

- Have students read the novel *The Wright 3* by Blue Balliett. The novel is a sequel to the captivating mystery, *Chasing Vermeer*. The story revolves around unexplainable accidents occurring at a Frank Lloyd Wright house, and three young gifted protagonists attempt to solve the mysteries. One of the main characters is obsessed with 3D pentominoes, and many mathematical patterns occur throughout the book.

Name: _____ Date: _____

Polygons on the Floor (Handout 9A)

Directions: At the Charlotte Douglas International Airport in Charlotte, NC, the terminal has a geometric pattern on the floor. It looks like the drawing shown below. Use tracing paper to trace and copy all of the different polygons that you can find. Write the name of each polygon on each drawing.

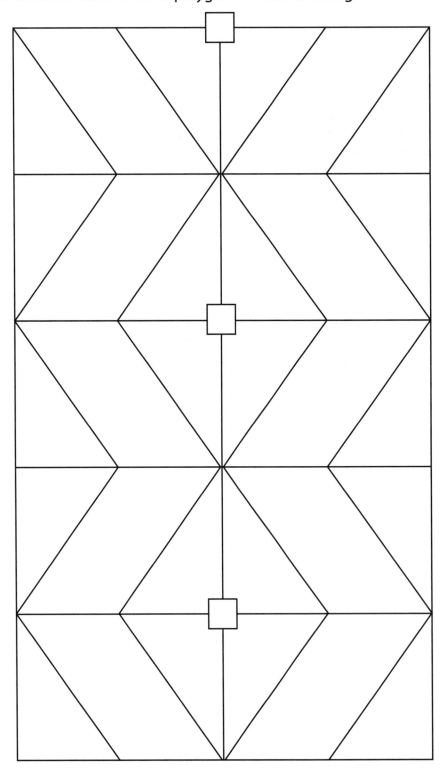

Polygons on the Floor Answer Key (Teacher Resource 1)

Directions: At the Charlotte Douglas International Airport in Charlotte, NC, the terminal has a geometric pattern on the floor. It looks like the drawing shown below. Use tracing paper to trace and copy all of the different polygons that you can find. Write the name of each polygon on each drawing.

Here are a number of possible polygons. Other polygons are also possible.

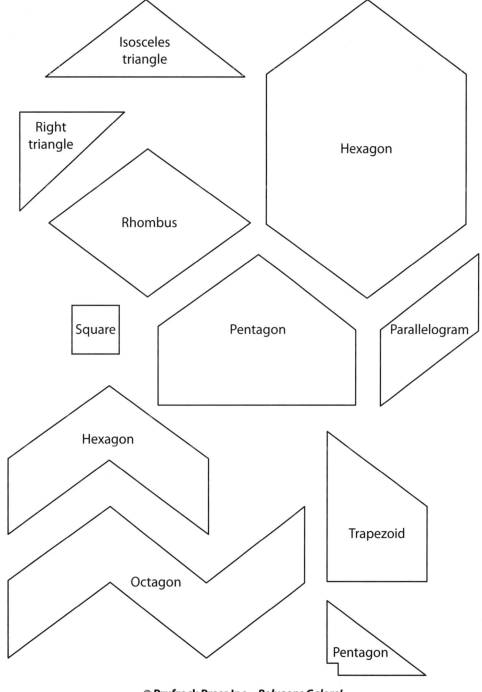

Name: _____ Date: _____

Polygons and Polyhedra Are Everywhere (Handout 9B)

Directions: Your task is to find examples of polygons and polyhedra in the real world. You may use any source including magazines, the Internet, newspapers, books, or observation of your surroundings. Try to find at least one example from each category. If you can, document your findings with a picture of the item. Otherwise, make a sketch or write a description.

Category	Name of Polygon or Polyhedron	Where Was the Item Found?	Sketch or Description
Architecture			
Art (e.g., painting, sculpture)			
Sports			
Fabric			
Inside a house			

Category	Name of Polygon or Polyhedron	Where Was the Item Found?	Sketch or Description
Food products			
Packaging			
Logos of corporations			
Nature			
Other			

Postassessment

Instructional Purpose

- To assess student knowledge and understanding of unit topics.

Materials and Handouts

- Postassessment

Activities

1. Distribute the **Postassessment** and have students complete it individually. Collect and score the assessments using the **Postassessment Answer Key**.

2. Have students compare their preassessment to their postassessment responses. In discussion, reflect upon what they have learned and how they have grown as mathematicians throughout the course of the unit.

Notes to Teacher

- The postassesssment is parallel in structure to the preassessment for this unit. Change any sets of questions to mirror any changes you made in the preassessment.

Postassessment

Directions: Do your best to answer the following questions.

1. Describe as many of each triangle's properties as you can.

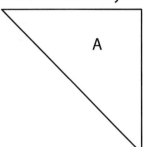
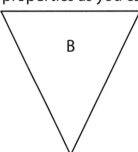

2. Group these triangles in any way you choose. Write the letters of the triangles in each group. Explain why you grouped them the way you did.

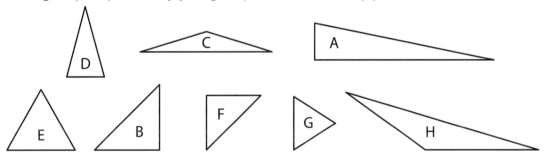

3. Danielle made a triangle out of three sticks. One stick was 10 inches long. Another was 12 inches long. What is true about the length of the third side of the triangle?

4. Given the figures at the right, write the letter of each that is a:

   a. quadrilateral _____

   b. rectangle _____

   c. parallelogram _____

   d. rhombus _____

   e. trapezoid _____

   f. kite _____

   g. square _____

   h. dart _____

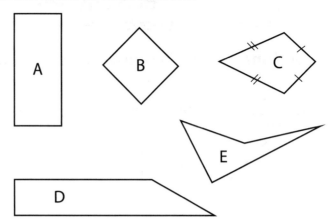

5. Without using a formula, find the area of this parallelogram. Explain your reasoning.

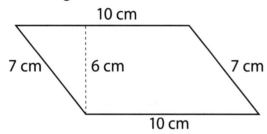

6. Look at this geometric figure.

   a. Is this figure a polygon? Explain why or why not.

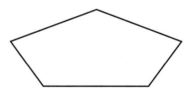

   b. Is it regular? Explain why or why not.

   c. What special name does this shape have?

7. A picture of a polyhedron is shown.

   a. How many faces does it have? _____

   b. How many vertices does it have? _____

   c. How many edges does it have? _____

8. Which of the items listed below is a polygon? _____

   Which is a polyhedron? _____

   a. A can of soup
   b. The top of a can of soup
   c. A shoe box
   d. The label from a can of soup

Postassessment Answer Key

Directions: Do your best to answer the following questions.

1. **(4 points)** Describe as many of each triangle's properties as you can.

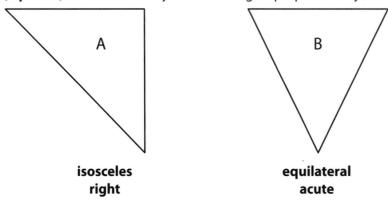

isosceles
right

equilateral
acute

Give one point for each correct response.

2. **(4 points)** Group these triangles in any way you choose. Write the letters of the triangles in each group. Explain why you grouped them the way you did.

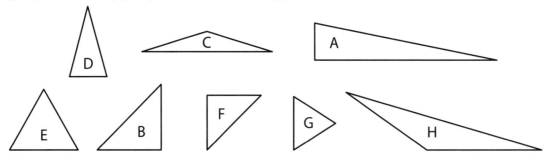

Many different groupings are possible. Each of the eight letters should be included in a group. The groups need not be labeled with technical terms but should have some description of what they have in common. Some examples of groupings are listed below.

Grouped by angles:	Grouped by whether it has a right angle or not:	Grouped by sides:
A, B, F (right triangles) D, E, G (acute triangles) C, H (obtuse triangles)	A, B, F (has a right angle) C, D, E, G, H (has no right angle)	E, G (equilateral) B, C, D, F, H (isosceles) A (scalene)

- **Give 4 points** if reasonable grouping is used, explanation of groups is given, terminology is correct, and all eight triangles are included in one group each.
- **Give 3 points** if groupings seem to be made based on characteristics of the triangles such as sides or angles but one of these is a problem:
  o   one or more triangles are left out,
  o   there is no adequate labeling of groups or explanation,
  o   terminology is primitive or incorrect (e.g., "square corners" instead of "right angles"), or
  o   the same triangle is included in more than one category.

- **Give 2 points** if the groupings are made based on visual characteristics such as "large and small" or "pointing right and pointing left" rather than using geometric terms as sorting categories.
- **Give 1 point** if there is minimal evidence of a sorting rule used but it is not totally correct or complete.
- **Give 0 points** if there is no response or if the student seems confused. Give 0 points if the sort is done by letters such as the vowels and consonants that are used to label them.

3. **(3 points)** Danielle made a triangle out of three sticks. One stick was 10 inches long. Another was 12 inches long. What is true about the length of the third side of the triangle?
    It must be more than 2 inches and less than 22 inches.

4. **(4 points)** Given the figures at the right, write the letter of each that is a:
    a. quadrilateral **A, B, C, D, E**
    b. rectangle **A, B**
    c. parallelogram **A, B**
    d. rhombus **B**
    e. trapezoid **D**
    f. kite **C**
    g. square **B**
    h. dart **E**

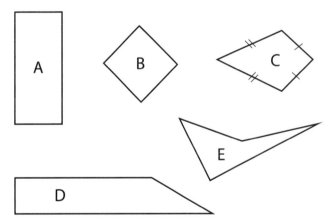

5. **(3 points)** Without using a formula, find the area of this parallelogram. Explain your reasoning.

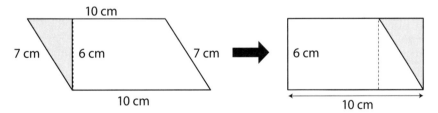

The area is 60 square cm. Move the triangle on the left to the right as shown and find the area of the rectangle or add the area of the two triangles to the area of the smaller rectangle.

6. **(3 points)** Look at this geometric figure.

    a. Is this figure a polygon? Explain why or why not.
   Yes, it satisfies the definition of a polygon because it is made of more than two line segments that do not intersect (except at endpoints), it lies in a plane, and it is closed.

    b. Is it regular? Explain why or why not.
   No. Not all of the sides and angles have the same measure.

    c. What special name does this shape have?
   Hexagon

7. **(3 points)** A picture of a polyhedron is shown.

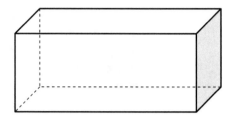

    a. How many faces does it have?
   6 faces

    b. How many vertices does it have?
   8 vertices

    c. How many edges does it have?
   12 edges

8. **(4 points)** Which of the items listed below is a polygon? **d**
   Which is a polyhedron? **c**

    a. A can of soup
    b. The top of a can of soup
    c. A shoe box
    d. The label from a can of soup

References

Balliett, B. (2005). *Chasing Vermeer*. New York, NY: Scholastic.

Balliett, B. (2006). *The Wright 3*. New York, NY: Scholastic.

Common Core State Standards Initiative. (2010). *The standards: Mathematics*. Retrieved from http://www.corestandards.org/assets/CCSSI_Math%20Standards.pdf

Crowley, M. L. (1987). The van Hiele model of the development of geometric thought. In M. M. Lindquist (Ed.), *Learning and teaching geometry, K–12* (pp. 1–16). Reston, VA: National Council of Teachers of Mathematics.

Jacobs, H. (1982). *Mathematics: A Human Endeavor*. New York, NY: W. H. Freeman & Co.

Mason, M. (1997). The van Hiele model of geometric understanding and mathematically talented students. *Journal for the Education of the Gifted, 21,* 38–53.

National Council of Teachers of Mathematics. (2000). *Principles and standards for school mathematics*. Reston, VA: Author.

Reimer, L., & Reimer, W. (1990). *Mathematicians Are People, Too: Stories From the Lives of Great Mathematicians*. Palo Alto, CA: Dale Seymour Publications.

Van Hiele, P. M. (1999). Developing geometric thinking through activities that begin with play. *Teaching Children Mathematics, 5,* 310–316.

About the Authors

Jill Adelson, Ph.D., is an assistant professor in the educational psychology, measurement, and evaluation program at the University of Louisville. She earned her Ph.D. in educational psychology with a joint emphasis in gifted education and in measurement, evaluation, and assessment from the University of Connecticut, and she earned her master's in curriculum and instruction with an emphasis in gifted education from The College of William and Mary. During her time in Virginia, she taught fourth grade self-contained gifted and talented. Dr. Adelson's research interests include the application of advanced statistical methods to examine issues in gifted and mathematics education, including the effects of gifted programming and elementary students' attitudes toward mathematics.

Dana T. Johnson teaches in the Mathematics Department and the School of Education at The College of William and Mary. In her early teaching career she taught middle and high school mathematics. She has worked on many projects with the Center for Gifted Education at William and Mary since its beginning, including curriculum development and professional development. Dana is the author of "Mathematics Curriculum for Gifted Learners" in *Comprehensive Curriculum for Gifted Learners* and "Adapting Mathematics Curricula for Gifted and Talented Learners" in *Content-Based Curriculum for High-Ability Learners*. She has a special interest in helping students develop spatial reasoning skills.

Marguerite M. Mason, Ph.D., is a professor of curriculum and instruction in the School of Education at The College of William and Mary. She specializes in the preparation of preservice and inservice teachers in mathematics education.